WATCHING WAITING

A 40-DAY END TIMES DEVOTIONAL

JACK HIBBS

BroadStreet
PUBLISHING

BroadStreet Publishing Group, LLC.
Savage, Minnesota, USA
Broadstreetpublishing.com

Watching Waiting: 40 Devotions for Living in the End Times
© 2025 Jack Hibbs

9781424571048
9781424571055 (eBook)

All rights reserved. No part of this publication may be reproduced, distributed, or transmitted in any form or by any means, including photocopying, recording, or other electronic or mechanical methods, without the prior written permission of the publisher, except in the case of brief quotations embodied in critical reviews and certain other noncommercial uses permitted by copyright law. No portion of this book may be used or reproduced in any way for the purpose of training artificial intelligence technologies. As per Article 4(3) of the Digital Single Market Directive 2019/790, BroadStreet Publishing reserves this work from the text and data mining exception.

All Scripture quotations are from the New King James Version®. Copyright © 1982 by Thomas Nelson. Used by permission. All rights reserved.

Requests for information should be addressed to:

> Real Life with Jack Hibbs
> P.O. Box 1273
> Chino Hills, CA 91709

www.jackhibbs.com

Typesetting and design by Garborg Design Works | garborgdesign.com
Editorial services by Michelle Winger | literallyprecise.com

Printed in China.

25 26 27 28 29 30 31   7 6 5 4 3 2 1

Faith, Hope, and Love

Speaking of the future, Paul wrote in 1 Corinthians 13:12-13, "For now we see in a mirror, dimly, but then face to face. Now I know in part, but then I shall know just as I also am known. And now abide faith, hope, love, these three; but the greatest of these is love."

Love is central to our faith, and it's the starting point of every devotion we will read together in this book. In Matthew 22:37-40, when asked which commandment was the greatest, Jesus replied, "'You shall love the Lord your God with all your heart, with all your soul, and with all your mind.' This is the first and great commandment. And the second is like it: 'You shall love your neighbor as yourself.' On these two commandments hang all the Law and the Prophets."

As we read about Bible prophecy over the next 40 days, it's crucial to keep in mind the bedrock principles of faith, hope, and love. They are the pillars that hold up our understanding and growth as believers. Especially love. Love for God and others forms the essence of Christian living and is the driving force behind our beliefs and actions.

This love that Jesus speaks of is not a natural human trait but a gift from God. It empowers us to love even those who oppose us. It is a heavenly love that transcends all human circumstances and surpasses all human understanding. This love is the foundation of everything we will explore in these devotions.

Remember, at the core of every teaching, at the center of every Bible prophecy, is the truth that God loves you, has hope for you, and desires for your faith to grow. Each devotion is written with the express purpose of strengthening your faith, bolstering your hope, and deepening your love for God and others.

So, as you journey through these 40 devotions, let faith, hope, and love be like a compass that guides your travels.

Why 40? The number 40 is significant in the Bible, indicating periods of testing, trial, and *transformation*. God caused it to rain for 40 days during the time of Noah (Genesis 7:12). Moses spent 40 days on Mount Sinai receiving the Law (Exodus 24:18). The Israelites wandered in the desert for 40 years before entering the Promised Land (Numbers 14:33-34). Jesus fasted for 40 days in the wilderness, where He was tempted by the devil (Matthew 4:1-2). Jesus appeared to His disciples over 40 days before ascending to heaven (Acts 1:3).

These periods of 40 are transformational times used by God to shape His people. As you engage with these 40 devotions, my prayer is that they alter the trajectory of your life. In fact—fair warning—I wouldn't be surprised if the next 40 days hold some intense trials and troubles for you! But as you focus on what is to come in *the Last Days*, my hope is that it will affect how you live, think, and speak in *these days*.

May the next 40 days be like a crucible that burns off all the distractions, delusions, deceptions, and other impurities of this world to purify us and sanctify us, so that we may be presented as the Bride of Christ when He comes: clean and bright, and arrayed in fine linen, which is the righteous acts of the saints (Revelation 19:7-8). Let us watch and wait with eager anticipation for the glorious day when He will come for us!

God bless you, my friend.
Awaiting His Return,

Jack Hibbs

Day 1

Be On the Watch

"Blessed are those servants whom the master, when he comes, will find watching."

Luke 12:37

Over and over again in Scripture, we are exhorted to be on the watch:

- Watch, stand fast in the faith, be brave, be strong. —1 Corinthians 16:13
- "Remember therefore how you have received and heard; hold fast and repent. Therefore if you will not watch, I will come upon you as a thief, and you will not know what hour I will come upon you." —Revelation 3:3
- "Take heed, watch and pray; for you do not know when the time is. It is like a man going to a far country, who left his house and gave authority to his servants, and to each his work, and commanded the doorkeeper to watch. Watch therefore, for you do not know when the master of the house is coming—in the evening,

at midnight, at the crowing of the rooster, or in the morning—lest, coming suddenly, he find you sleeping. And what I say to you, I say to all: Watch!" —Mark 13:33-37

That word *watch* or *watching* appears in the New Testament many more times as well, and it appears in three different forms. In English, it's the word *watch*, but in the Greek language, we find three manifestations of that word.

1. *Gregoreuo*: to keep awake, literally and/or figuratively, to be in a state of vigilance, being watchful, on the alert, to keep watch.
2. *Tereo*: to set a guard, to continue the watch or the guard, to be the guardian, to be keeping your eyes open and on the horizon.
3. *Agrupneo*: to be sleepless, wakeful: be on the alert (1), keep on the alert (2), keep watch, custody (3), observe (4), preserve.

That's how we as believers are to be living—vigilantly. We're to be awake and we're to be on guard, looking at the horizon for things to come. We are to persevere, to stay at it, to not give up. Living a life of vigilance requires consistent effort and dedication so that we remain prepared for what lies ahead. This means our faith is not passive, but that we make an active commitment to live what we believe and stand in readiness for the return of Jesus. More than ever before the Church needs to be at her post, fully awake, ready to receive the coming of the Lord Jesus and in the meantime be busy about the Father's business.

The three definitions for that one word, *watch*, can be summed up in this: always be waiting.

We are to be watching so that we are in the mindset of eagerly waiting.

If you are watching and waiting for the Lord Jesus Christ, your spiritual walk will shape up quickly. Most of us can readily admit that we need to get into shape physically. We know that it takes effort and diligence to stay fit. But when we finally take the steps to get our bodies into shape, we feel better.

When you get into shape, things don't hold you back and you can accomplish more. The same is true spiritually. When we are in a watchful, waiting mindset, we are training our spiritual selves to be fit—ready at a moment's notice to spring into action, and anticipating the Lord's return with eagerness.

Questions for Thought or Discussion

Personal Vigilance

How can you apply the concept of *gregoreuo* in your daily life to remain spiritually awake and vigilant? Can you share a specific practice or habit that helps you stay alert in your faith?

Guarding Your Faith

The term *tereo* emphasizes setting a guard and being a guardian. What practical steps can you take to guard your heart and mind against distractions and spiritual complacency? How can you encourage other believers to do the same?

Living with Eagerness

Agrupneo speaks to being constantly alert and watchful. How does living with the expectation of Christ's return influence your daily actions and decisions? How can this mindset help you stay focused on your spiritual growth?

Let's Pray

Heavenly Father,

Thank You for reminding us to stay vigilant and watchful. Help us to be alert and ready for Your return, guarding our hearts and minds against distractions. Strengthen us to live each day with purpose and anticipation, working to be spiritually fit and eager to do Your will. Give us discernment to recognize the signs of Your coming and to remain steadfast in our faith until then.

In Jesus' name we pray. Amen.

Day 2

We Interrupt This Broadcast...

"Now when these things begin to happen, look up and lift up your heads, because your redemption draws near."

Luke 21:28

If you are old enough, you remember the days when we would watch ABC, CBS, or NBC—those were our only choices—and suddenly, the screen would get staticky or go blank, followed by this message: "We interrupt this broadcast to bring you this special report."

For those of you who are young, you might find it hard to imagine. It didn't happen very often, but when you saw your TV show interrupted with that message, something big was about to be announced, and you'd stop dead in your tracks to find out what it was.

Some of those moments left a lasting imprint on our minds. We can remember where we were, what we were wearing, even the weather. For example, I remember my mom coming to my school upset. Back then, parents would pick up their kids from school. I vividly remember that she had on a red blouse, and I can picture her crying, which shook me. She told me, "They've just killed the president. The president's been killed." That was November 22, 1963, in Dallas, Texas. Do you remember that?

What about July 20, 1969? I stood in the front yard with my dad and brother. My dad pointed to the moon and said, "You see that? There's a man stepping onto the moon *right now*." As young as I was, I didn't care much, but as I grew up, I understood how significant that was.

Many of us in Southern California will never forget February 9, 1971. At exactly 6:00 am and one second, Sylmar was struck by a major earthquake. Parts of Los Angeles collapsed, and the shaking was incredible. Schools in Orange County were closed for several weeks because of the tremors. I remember running down the hallway to my parents' bedroom, crashing into the walls because the hallway was moving so much.

Another unforgettable day was January 28, 1986. The Challenger space shuttle exploded, and we lost our astronauts. None of us will ever forget that image on our television screens.

It seemed like the entire United States had perfectly clear weather on Tuesday, September 11, 2001. I remember waking up, having my coffee, and turning on the TV. I stood there and watched my nation change in a moment as the Twin Towers collapsed from being hit by airplanes controlled by terrorists.

Listen, my friend. The volume of major events happening in the world around us is increasing and will continue to do so exponentially as the Day of Christ draws closer. These "we interrupt this broadcast" moments will become more frequent, like birth pangs. Jesus Christ Himself said, "Now when these things begin to happen, look up and lift up your heads, because your redemption draws near."

Why did Jesus tell us to look up as things grow more chaotic, intense, and eventful in this world? So that we believers can walk more boldly, more informed, and more ready to not only share Christ with others, but to meet the Lord Jesus when He comes.

Questions for Thought or Discussion

Reflecting on Moments of Impact
Think about a significant event in your life that left a lasting impression, similar to those mentioned (JFK's assassination, the moon landing, a California earthquake, 9/11). How did that event change your perspective? How did it affect your faith?

Recognizing Modern Interruptions
In today's world, we're often bombarded with breaking news and major events. How do you discern which events are significant in the context of your faith? How can you stay focused on God's message amid the noise?

Preparing for the Future

Jesus instructed us to "look up and lift up our heads because redemption draws near." How can you prepare yourself spiritually and mentally for the increasing frequency of "we interrupt this broadcast" moments? What steps can you take to ensure you're ready to share Christ in these times?

Let's Pray

Heavenly Father,

Thank You for being with us in these uncertain times. Help us stay focused on You while this world is in chaos. Remind us to look up and remember Your promise of redemption. Give us boldness and courage to stand firm in our faith and share Your hope with others. Prepare our hearts for Your return and help us live with purpose and urgency. Fill us with Your peace and help us to be a light to those around us.

In Jesus' name we pray. Amen.

Day 3

As Evil Increases

Wait for [God's] Son from heaven, whom He raised from the dead, even Jesus who delivers us from the wrath to come.
1 Thessalonians 1:10

I was interviewed by a media group in New York City, and they asked me this question: "Why does it seem like there's so much evil going on in our nation and world today?" Can you believe it? A secular organization asking a pastor about the state of evil in the world; it's an indicator of the times we're living in.

Evil is becoming so prominent that even the world is sitting up and taking notice. But everything is falling right into place according to God's calendar, and the only way we'll understand it is if we understand God's Word. The world is starting to panic, and if you weren't a Christian, you'd be just like them: either trying to figure it out or getting drunk in an attempt to ignore it.

In times like these, it is crucial for believers to stay grounded in their faith and immersed in Scripture. The Bible not only foretells these events but also provides the assurance that God is in control. By staying connected to His Word, we can navigate these evil days with a sense of peace and direction that the world desperately lacks.

Jesus said that chaotic days would come upon the earth—so chaotic that men's hearts would fail them. In John 14:29, Jesus said, "And now I have told you before it comes, that when it does come to pass, you may believe." These days we're experiencing were foretold by Jesus, and the Bible has an urgent message for every generation of Christians: be faithful, watch, and be ready for Christ's return.

We must understand that the increasing evil is not outside of God's knowledge or control. He is sovereign and has foreseen all things. As believers, we are called to be light in the darkness and to trust in His promises, knowing that His wrath is reserved for the wicked, not for His faithful followers.

The wrath that is mentioned in today's verse is the vengeance of God described in Bible prophecy as the seven-year tribulation period. God promises in this verse to deliver true believers from His wrath.

This is an exciting time to be alive, to say the least. If you ever felt like you should have been born at a different time, know that your existence here and now is not a mistake; you're here for such a time as this. You're a believer at this time because God has a purpose for you.

I used to feel like I was born a couple of centuries too late, because I wanted to be part of the colonial revolutionary period in America. I thought I had to settle for the fact that God placed me here. But perhaps that spirit is within me because He wants to use me to do something revolutionary today!

We are called to be warriors for Christ in this age, standing firm against the tide of evil and spreading His truth. Our mission is clear: to make disciples of all nations and to stand as ambassadors of His hope and righteousness.

Let's shake up the kingdom of hell. Let's cause some trouble among the forces of darkness and evil. The Bible says that by our obedience to Christ, we punish disobedience (2 Corinthians 10:6). Evil should shudder and shake when you worship God and shine your light.

Questions for Thought or Discussion

Awareness of Evil

How do you personally perceive the increase of evil in the world today? How does this awareness affect your daily life and interactions with others?

Response to Chaos

In the face of chaotic events and increasing evil, what verses and promises help you maintain hope and confidence in God's plan? How does your faith influence your response to uncertainties?

Purpose in the Present

Reflecting on the idea of being born "for such a time as this," what do you believe is your purpose in the current day and age? How can you actively fulfill this purpose in your daily life and interactions with others?

Let's Pray

Heavenly Father,

In a world darkened by increasing evil, we turn to You for strength and guidance. Help us to trust in Your plan and to shine Your light into the darkness. Empower us to fulfill our purpose in this present age, spreading Your love and truth wherever we go. As we eagerly await the return of Your Son, may we be steadfast in faith and bold in action. Use us to bring hope and help to a hurting world.

In Jesus' name we pray. Amen.

Day 4

Be Vigilant

Christ was offered once to bear the sins of many. To those who eagerly wait for Him He will appear a second time, apart from sin, for salvation.

Hebrews 9:28

Jesus died once—that's all He needed to do—to bear the sins of many. And to those who eagerly wait for Him, He will appear a second time. Are you waiting for Him?

In my opinion, this verse ties a bow on the believer's life. Jesus Christ died on the cross once, and He will never have to die again. His salvation for you is all you need.

And in response to this amazing truth, we should be eagerly waiting for Him to come again. Some pastors or teachers might say otherwise, casting doubt. They might argue that the prophecies regarding His second coming are merely symbolic or that they have already been fulfilled in some way. Watch out for people who say, "I don't think the Lord could come back." It doesn't matter if it's a celebrity or a respected Bible teacher or a religious guru or any other person of interest. The Bible says we are to be eagerly waiting for His return, and the Bible holds all authority when it comes to truth.

The next time someone says to you, "Jesus isn't coming back. People have been saying He's coming back for centuries," take a selfie with them and post that you just met someone fulfilling Bible prophecy. That person is what the Bible foretold of in 2 Peter 3:3-4, where it says: "Scoffers will come in the last days, walking according to their own lusts, and saying, 'Where is the promise of His coming? For since the fathers fell asleep, all things continue as they were from the beginning of creation.'"

We are to be watching and waiting for Christ to appear a second time. You might ask, "What if somebody's not looking for Him?" A true believer will have in his or her theology that the coming of the Lord Jesus could be at any time. Even if they're backslidden, they know He could come whenever. It's always interesting to see backslidden Christians biting their fingernails, panicking and terrified about everything in the news. Why? Because they are living outside the will of God. They are children of heaven, but they aren't walking with God, so they are miserable. They are not ready.

Don't be messing around with sin and playing with the fire of temptation when He comes, because you don't want to be ashamed at His appearing. Can you imagine if Christ came today and you were a believer who wasn't ready? The shame you would feel in doing what you knew you shouldn't—or not doing what you knew you should—would be very real.

Christ died once for our sins. That should be enough to motivate us to live wholeheartedly devoted to Him: watching and waiting for His second appearing.

As believers, our readiness for Christ's return should permeate every aspect of our lives. It should influence our choices, our relationships, and our priorities. Let's not be complacent or distracted by the cares of this world, but instead, let's eagerly anticipate His coming and live in a manner worthy of His calling.

Questions for Thought or Discussion

Eager Anticipation
How does the promise of Christ's return impact your daily life and decisions? Are there specific ways you can cultivate a mindset of eagerly waiting for His second coming?

Spiritual Readiness
What does it mean to be spiritually ready for Christ's return? How can you ensure you are not caught unprepared or ashamed at His appearing?

Responding to Scoffers
How do you respond to those who scoff at the idea of Christ's return, as mentioned in 2 Peter 3:3-4? How can

you stay firm in your faith and encourage others to remain vigilant despite skepticism and doubt?

Let's Pray

Heavenly Father,

Thank You for the promise of Christ's return. Help us to live each day with eager anticipation, staying vigilant and ready. Strengthen our faith so we can stand firm against doubt and skepticism. Guide us to live wholeheartedly for You, always watching and waiting. May our lives reflect the hope we have in Your Son's imminent return, leading others to the salvation that is only found in Him.

In Jesus' name we pray. Amen.

Day 5

Our Heavenly Citizenship

Our citizenship is in heaven, from which we also eagerly wait for the Savior, the Lord Jesus Christ.
Philippians 3:20

If your faith is securely anchored in Jesus Christ, your citizenship is not in this world but in heaven. Spiritually speaking, you have a passport that is issued by heaven, and you eagerly await the day you get to go home.

Recently, my American passport expired, so I had to get it renewed. This meant I had to get a new photo taken.

When I pulled out the old passport and compared its photo from ten years ago to the one I had just taken, I felt like I was looking at a completely different person! In the new picture, I had extra skin and lots of wrinkles. My ears are twice as long as they were ten years ago, and my nose is getting bigger! (Don't tell me there's no curse or Satan or hell when your ears keep growing and your nose keeps getting bigger. We're definitely in a broken world!)

As I looked at my passport, I thought, *This may get me in and out of America, but thank God my real citizenship is in heaven. And in my heavenly passport, I look just like Jesus!*

Is your citizenship in heaven? If so, the Bible says that you reflect the righteousness of Christ that's been imparted to you. That's a good thing. No one's going to have big noses and long ears in heaven. All the remnants of sin will be taken away. Instead, our images will reflect the righteousness of the One who gave His life for us to be there.

What does heavenly citizenship mean for us?

1. Eternal Blessings and Inheritance

As citizens of heaven, we are not only assured of eternal life, but we are also inheritors of God's promises. Scripture speaks of an inheritance that is imperishable, undefiled, and unfading, kept in heaven for us (1 Peter 1:4). This inheritance includes not only the joys of eternity but also the rewards of faithful service here on earth (Matthew 25:21).

2. Abiding in God's Presence

Our heavenly citizenship means that when we die, we will be in the presence of God Himself. Revelation 21:3 describes God dwelling among His people, wiping away every tear from their eyes. This eternal communion with our Creator should fill us with immeasurable joy and thanksgiving.

3. Participating in God's Kingdom

Citizenship in heaven means active participation in God's eternal kingdom. We are not passive spectators but co-laborers with Christ in His work of redemption. Our work here on earth is to proclaim God's kingdom by sharing the message of salvation with the world.

4. Becoming More Like Christ

Our heavenly citizenship involves a process of being transformed into the likeness of Christ. As we walk through life, the Holy Spirit works within us to conform us to the image of God's Son (Romans 8:29). This sanctifying work prepares us for our eternal home, where we will bear the resemblance of Jesus so much more than we do now. Paul told the Thessalonian church, "Now may the God of peace Himself sanctify you completely; and may your whole spirit, soul, and body be preserved blameless at the coming of our Lord Jesus Christ." (1 Thessalonians 5:23)

5. Unity with the Body of Christ

Being citizens of heaven also means being part of the global Body of Christ, which transcends race, nationality, and culture. Our shared identity as children of God allows us to work in unity here on earth. In heaven, that unity and fellowship with believers from all over the world will be perfected.

Reflecting on these aspects of heavenly citizenship should motivate us to live in a manner worthy of our calling. When you consider that your true citizenship is in heaven, it will make your waiting and watching all the more eager!

Questions for Thought or Discussion

Heavenly Citizenship

How does knowing that your true citizenship is in heaven impact your life today? In what ways does this perspective influence your decisions, priorities, and interactions with others?

Eagerly Waiting

What does it mean to "eagerly wait for the Savior" as described in Philippians 3:20? How can you practically live with anticipation and readiness for Christ's return?

Our Heavenly Identity

In what ways does the assurance of heavenly citizenship provide comfort and hope in difficult times? How has this truth helped you navigate personal struggles and the brokenness of the world?

Let's Pray

Heavenly Father,

Thank You for the reminder that our true citizenship is in heaven. Help us to live each day with the awareness of our eternal home, eagerly awaiting the return of our Savior, Jesus Christ. Strengthen us to reflect His righteousness in all we do and to find comfort and hope in our heavenly identity. Empower us to be faithful, watchful, and ready for His return.

In Jesus' name we pray. Amen.

Day 6

One World

The beast which I saw was like a leopard, his feet were like the feet of a bear, and his mouth like the mouth of a lion. The dragon gave him his power, his throne, and great authority. And I saw one of his heads as if it had been mortally wounded, and his deadly wound was healed. And all the world marveled and followed the beast. So they worshiped the dragon who gave authority to the beast; and they worshiped the beast, saying, "Who is like the beast? Who is able to make war with him?
Revelation 13:2-4

The Bible warns us that the world will be united under the leadership of the Antichrist. The Church will be raptured before then, but we are witnesses now of the trends and steps leading to the formation of this coming new world order. Even in today's news we can see the push toward a one-world government, one-world faith, and one-world currency. We see these developments unfolding today, highlighting the urgency of being spiritually aware and vigilant.

One-World Government and Faith

We are witnessing a growing push for global unity, both politically and religiously. World leaders and influential figures are increasingly calling for a unified global government and a consolidated faith system. This might seem like a noble effort to achieve peace and harmony especially in a world rife with conflict and division. But the Bible cautions us that these efforts are rooted in deceptive, satanic origins. In Revelation 13, it is prophesied that a global leader will rise, uniting the world under his authority. This leader, the Antichrist, will deceive many by promising peace and security, but his true intentions are sinister.

As believers, we must be discerning and not be swayed by these global movements. Our allegiance is to Christ alone, and we must stand firm in our faith, recognizing that true unity and peace will only be achieved under the reign of Jesus Christ.

One-World Economy and Currency

Economic instability is another sign pointing to the End Times. Calls for a new economic system and a unified global currency are becoming more prevalent. The Bible predicts that such an economic shift will be part of the Antichrist's strategy to exert control and lead people astray. In Revelation 13:16-17, it is foretold that the Antichrist will implement a system where no one can buy or sell without a specific mark, symbolizing absolute economic control.

This push for a one-world currency is already evident in the discussions of major economic forums and organizations. The current economic turmoil, coupled with the search for stability, is paving the way for such a system to be accepted by the masses. As Christians, we must remain steadfast and rely on God's provision, knowing that He will sustain us through any economic challenges.

Living in Expectation

As believers, we're called to watch and be ready for Christ's appearing. Recognizing these global trends should prompt us to hold fast to our faith and live with a sense of urgency and purpose. Our true citizenship is in heaven, and we should eagerly await the return of our Savior, Jesus Christ. This anticipation should influence our daily lives, driving us to live in a way that honors God and reflects His love to the world.

Knowing that these signs were foretold in the Bible should not cause us to fear but to have hope and confidence in God's sovereign plan. Jesus Himself said, "Now when these things begin to happen, look up and lift up your heads, because your redemption draws near....Watch therefore, and pray always that you may be counted worthy to escape all these things that will come to pass, and to stand before the Son of Man" (Luke 21:28, 36). This is a time for us to be vigilant, faithful, and ready for His return.

Questions for Thought or Discussion

One-World Government and Faith

What precursors to a one-world government or religion have you seen in recent news?

One World Economy and Currency

How are technology and social behavior/expectations setting the stage for a one-world economy and currency?

Living in Expectation

How should the knowledge of your heavenly citizenship influence your daily life and interactions with others in these unprecedented times?

Let's Pray

Heavenly Father,

We thank You for Your guidance and wisdom. As we see signs of global unity and economic shifts, help us stay vigilant and rooted in our faith. Strengthen us to discern truth from deception and to rely on Your provision. May our anticipation of Christ's return inspire us to live with purpose and reflect Your love. Keep us faithful and ready for the day of His appearing.

In Jesus' name we pray. Amen.

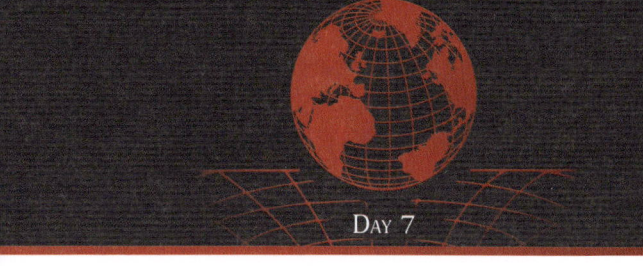

Day 7

Misinformation

Jesus answered and said to them: "Take heed that no one deceives you. For many will come in My name, saying, 'I am the Christ,' and will deceive many."

Matthew 24:4-5

In today's world, confusion and misinformation are rampant. With the rise of social media and new digital platforms, misinformation blurs the lines between truth and falsehood. Jesus warned us in Matthew 24:4-5 that deception would be a defining characteristic of the Last Days. He urged His followers to be vigilant and discerning, emphasizing the importance of staying grounded in truth.

Jesus' warning about deception is more relevant now than ever before. We live in an age where misinformation spreads rapidly through media and technology. It can be challenging to discern truth from falsehood, especially when many voices claim to have the answers. We saw this during the COVID panic, where conflicting information about the virus and its transmission caused fear and hysteria among the population. Self-labeled "experts" provided contradictory statements using "science" as a shield from any opposition, further complicating the situation and eroding people's trust.

Misinformation in political campaigns can manipulate public opinion, sway elections, and incite unrest. During election cycles, false narratives and fake news stories often circulate, leading to division and distrust among citizens. In times of war or conflict, propaganda and misinformation are frequently employed as tools to justify military actions or demonize opposing factions, making it difficult for people to separate fact from fiction.

Misinformation, disinformation, and confusion are tools that Satan uses to lead people astray, causing them to believe in false doctrines and ideologies. When you are not informed, you are misinformed. There is no void in the brain; if you don't have accurate information, misinformation fills the space.

The only way to guard against deception is by knowing God's Word. The Bible is our ultimate source of truth and our defense against lies. When we immerse ourselves in Scripture, we equip ourselves with the knowledge needed to discern truth from error. Without this foundation, we are vulnerable to being misled.

In a world where misinformation is so widespread, it's crucial to remain steadfast in our faith. This means continually seeking God's wisdom through prayer and the study of His Word and being cautious about the sources of information we trust. It's also important to engage with fellow believers, encouraging and supporting one another in our walk with Christ.

As believers, we should not be swayed by every new claim or doctrine that comes our way. Instead, we must test everything against the truth of God's Word. Like the Berean Jews in Acts 17:11, who "received the word with all readiness, and searched the Scriptures daily to find out whether these things were so," we too must diligently study the Scriptures and compare them with any teachings or beliefs presented to us.

Scripture is our ultimate authority. It is the living and active Word of God (Hebrews 4:12), inspired by the Holy Spirit. Its truths are timeless and unchanging, providing a solid foundation on which we can build our lives. By aligning our beliefs and actions with the teachings of Scripture, we align ourselves with God's will and wisdom, ensuring that we are not swayed by the shifting sands of human opinion or the deceptions of the enemy.

Questions for Thought or Discussion

Recognizing Deception

How can you identify deception in today's world, and what steps can you take to protect yourself from being misled?

Knowing the Bible

Why is it essential to have a strong understanding of the Bible in order to discern truth from falsehood? How can you deepen your knowledge of Scripture?

Standing Firm

In what ways can you support and encourage others to remain steadfast in their faith amid widespread confusion and misinformation?

Let's Pray

Heavenly Father,

We thank You for Your Word which is our source of truth and guidance. In a world filled with confusion and misinformation, help us to remain wary and discerning. Strengthen our faith and deepen our understanding of Scripture, so we can stand firm against deception. Guide us in encouraging one another to stay true to Your teachings. Give us discernment so we can navigate through the sea of misinformation and discern truth from falsehood. Empower us to spread Your light in the darkness. May we continually seek Your wisdom and rely on Your truth.

In Jesus' name we pray. Amen.

Day 8

Apostasy in the Last Days

The Spirit expressly says that in latter times some will depart from the faith, giving heed to deceiving spirits and doctrines of demons, speaking lies in hypocrisy, having their own conscience seared with a hot iron.

1 Timothy 4:1-2

The Holy Spirit is clear and direct in warning that in the latter times, some will depart from the faith. We are witnessing this in unprecedented numbers, with people abandoning their faith and family. People are walking away from their marriages, whether brand new or decades old, and individuals are renouncing their beliefs. This phenomenon is not limited to one area or church; it is widespread.

People are giving up on their faith, family, and commitments, often unexpectedly. This trend is alarming and unparalleled in any other time of Church history. It's as if there's an invisible lever people are willing to pull when things get tough, opting to bail out rather than persevere.

The deceiving spirits Jesus spoke of won't announce their intentions plainly. Instead, they will be subtle and appealing, much like how Satan deceived Eve. She was perfect, yet Satan's deception was so enticing that she chose it over God's truth. Deceiving spirits still work in the same way, implanting thoughts that seem harmless or appealing at first but lead us astray.

The allure of their lies draws many away from the absolute truths of Scripture. Deceiving spirits whisper lies disguised as enlightenment, luring people away from truth. False teachings and demonic doctrines undermine God's Word, sowing seeds of doubt and confusion among believers.

The lies that Satan and this culture spread propagate misinformation and confusion. They introduce ideas that seem innocent but are ultimately destructive.

Hypocrisy is prevalent as well, with people saying one thing but doing another. This double standard is evident in multiple aspects of life. Those who speak lies in hypocrisy impose restrictions on others while exempting themselves, showcasing a lack of integrity and a seared conscience. They can't feel anything anymore. It's the perfect description of a narcissist. They lack empathy, sympathy, love, and heart. They can't feel the pain or needs of others, only focusing on their own desires. This lack of compassion is a clear sign of a seared conscience.

In these days of deception, the need for discernment and steadfastness in the faith cannot be overstated. Believers must be vigilant against the subtle deceptions that permeate society, guarding their hearts and minds with the truth of Scripture. By immersing themselves in the Word of God and deepening their relationship with Him, they can withstand the onslaught of falsehood and remain rooted in the unchanging truth of the Bible.

Know this: in these Last Days, you will see increased attacks on your thinking coming from deceiving spirits, invisible entities that will lie to you. Your only defense against spiritual deception is having Scripture embedded in your spirit. If you don't know the Bible, you're susceptible to deception.

Remember, everything we read in Scripture has already been tested, tried, and attacked. Yet here we are, reading statements made 2,000 years ago that fit perfectly with tomorrow's news. This shows the timeless relevance of God's Word.

Questions for Thought or Discussion

Apostasy
Without naming names, have you witnessed people falling away from the church—maybe someone you would never have guessed would do so? How can you

support those who are struggling with their faith to help prevent them from falling away?

Recognizing Deception

How can you identify subtle deceptions in your daily life and guard against them?

Knowing the Bible

Why is a strong understanding of the Bible crucial for discerning truth from falsehood? What are some practical steps you can take to deepen your knowledge of Scripture?

Let's Pray

Heavenly Father,

In a time of unprecedented confusion and deception, we seek Your truth and guidance. Protect our faith and help us support others who may be struggling. Implant in us a heart of discernment to recognize falsehood and deepen our knowledge of Your Word. Draw back those who have strayed and strengthen those on the brink of apostasy. Keep us humble and sincere, shining Your light in the darkness.

In Jesus' name we pray. Amen.

Day 9

Bible Prophecy Is Reliable

God is not a man, that He should lie,
Nor a son of man, that He should repent.
Has He said, and will He not do?
Or has He spoken, and will He not make it good?
NUMBERS 23:19

Everyone wants to know the future. Our world is cluttered with predictions and prophecies, and it's easy to become entangled in speculation about what lies ahead. From the enigmatic forecasts of Nostradamus to the modern-day prognosticators like Jeane Dixon, many claim to offer insights into the future.

Speaking of Nostradamus, it's been claimed that 71% of his predictions have come true… but have you read them? They are so vague. For example, "Seven months great war, people dead through evil." That's the prediction? That could be attached to any number of conflicts in our world, and it is still being applied to some today.

Here's another one he wrote: "Light on Mars falling." People are ready to apply any number of explanations to these words, from Elon Musk's plans for colonization to the deployment of NASA's rover on the Red Planet.

People are willing to believe any number of prophecies about the future and have itching ears when it comes to the "foretellings" of prophets, psychics, mystics, and fortunetellers. Yet, amid all of these, there stands one timeless source of truth and one perfect predictor of things to come: the Bible.

Scripture tells us in 2 Timothy 3:16 that "All Scripture is given by inspiration of God." Unlike the vague and often contradictory predictions of man, the Bible stands as a steadfast pillar of truth. Its prophecies, penned by holy men moved by the Holy Spirit, have withstood the test of time with unparalleled accuracy.

Consider the prophecies concerning the first coming of Jesus Christ. Over 300 prophecies foretold specific details about His birth, life, and death, all of which were fulfilled precisely as predicted. This remarkable fulfillment demonstrates that only God could have authored Scripture, and it underscores its reliability.

The Bible warns us repeatedly against false prophets and deceptive teachings. In 2 Peter 1:20-21, we're reminded that no prophecy of Scripture is of private interpretation and that holy men spoke as they were moved by the Holy Spirit. Unlike the prophecies of man, which often rely on subjective interpretation and guesswork, the Word of God is clear and authoritative.

The Bible transcends the limitations of time itself. Psalm 90:2 declares, "Before the mountains were brought forth, or ever You had formed the earth and the world, even from everlasting to everlasting, You are God." God is the father of time, governing its ebb and flow according to His divine purposes. In a world where uncertainty reigns and time slips through our fingers, we find assurance in the timeless truths of Scripture.

Why do we watch and wait for the return of Jesus Christ? Because we trust the words of Scripture. We don't have to guess what the future will hold because God has already told us, and we can anchor ourselves in His unchanging Word. His promises are steadfast, His wisdom is unshakable, and His truth is uncompromised.

Questions for Thought or Discussion

Prophecy Fulfilled
How do the fulfilled prophecies regarding the first coming of Jesus Christ strengthen your confidence in the reliability of Scripture regarding His second coming? What prophecies stand out to you the most?

Discerning Truth
In a world filled with predictions and prophecies, why is it important for believers to discern between the Word of God and the teachings of man? How can you guard

yourself against deceptive teachings and false prophets?

Eternal Perspective

Reflecting on Psalm 90:2, which declares God's eternal nature, how does this perspective on time influence your understanding of prophecy and God's sovereignty over the future? How does it impact your trust in His promises?

Let's Pray

Heavenly Father,

Thank You for the unchanging truth of Your Word. This world is filled with uncertainty and speculation, and we find comfort in knowing that Your promises are sure, and Your wisdom is unshakable. Help us to anchor ourselves in Your Word, trusting in Your faithfulness and sovereignty over all things. Give us discernment to distinguish between Your truth and the deceptive teachings of man. May we walk in confidence, knowing that Your Word stands forever.

In Jesus' name we pray. Amen.

Day 10

Affections of the End Times

Know this, that in the last days perilous times will come: For men will be lovers of themselves, lovers of money, boasters, proud, blasphemers, disobedient to parents, unthankful, unholy, unloving, unforgiving, slanderers, without self-control, brutal, despisers of good, traitors, headstrong, haughty, lovers of pleasure rather than lovers of God, having a form of godliness but denying its power. And from such people turn away!

2 Timothy 3:1-5

The affection of man's heart is a telltale sign of the times. The verses above paint a vivid picture of the characteristics that will mark the Last Days. It's astonishing to witness the accuracy of this 2,000-year-old prophecy unfolding before our very eyes.

In these perilous times, people will become lovers of themselves, consumed by self-centeredness and narcissism. The pursuit of wealth will drive their actions, overshadowing values of integrity and compassion. They will do absolutely anything—selling body, mind, or soul—if it will make them rich. They will boast in their achievements, truly believing they are superior. Pride is the banner that they fly, disregarding humility in any form.

Blasphemy has become increasingly common, with the disrespect of God expressed in both words and action. Disobedience to parents—or any authority figure—is prevalent, as people blatantly disregard and disparage them.

Ingratitude has become widespread to the point where whole generations are being labeled as "entitled," failing to appreciate the blessings and opportunities they have been given. Lack of holiness is evident in the moral decline and ethical compromises that characterize the culture around us.

Social media platforms serve as breeding grounds for slander and division, as individuals engage in unloving and unforgiving behavior. The absence of self-control leads to brutality and a disdain for goodness. Agreements are broken, trust is betrayed, and stubbornness prevails.

In all this, pleasure takes precedence over God. People find fulfillment in indulgence rather than in worshiping the Creator. They may attend church, but their lives deny the transformational power of true godliness.

Have you seen these characteristics growing in our population? Can you put faces to some of these labels:

boasters, disobedient to parents, headstrong, money lovers, or pleasure seekers? There is a self-focused, self-centered, self-absorbed movement that is exponentially increasing in speed.

We're living in a time when societal norms dictate what we are supposed to love, approve, and believe. You must love *this* agenda. You must approve of *that* lifestyle. You have to join the team and get onboard with what's socially acceptable. Those who dissent face ostracism and consequences. The workplace, once solely focused on qualifications, now demands adherence to social agendas. Where does this come from? Demonic influence in the lives of mankind.

As believers, we're called to resist conformity to the world's standards. Romans 12:1-2 instructs: "Present your bodies a living sacrifice, holy, acceptable to God, which is your reasonable service. And do not be conformed to this world, but be transformed by the renewing of your mind, that you may prove what is that good and acceptable and perfect will of God."

We must stand firm in our convictions, rooted in God's truth, even when faced with opposition. As we navigate these days when people are lovers of themselves, their wallets, and their diversions, let's remember that our ultimate allegiance is to God, not to the ever-changing dictates of culture. Let's cling to His Word and rely on His strength to uphold us.

Questions for Thought or Discussion

Man's Affections
Reflecting on 2 Timothy 3:1-5, how do the characteristics described in these verses resonate with the current state of society? What examples of these behaviors have you observed in the world around you?

Resisting Pressures
How can you maintain your convictions and stand firm in your faith amid the cultural pressures to conform? What biblical principles can guide you in navigating these challenges?

Personal Integrity
In what areas of your life do you feel the tension between societal expectations and biblical values? How can you uphold your integrity and remain faithful to God's truth in these areas?

Let's Pray

Heavenly Father,

Self-centeredness and societal pressures abound all around us! Help us to stand firm in our faith and convictions. Give us the courage to resist conformity to the patterns of this world and to remain steadfast in Your truth. May Your Word be our guide and Your

Spirit our strength as we encounter opposition in these Last Days. Empower us to live lives that honor You and bear witness to Your character.

In Jesus' name we pray. Amen.

Day 11

What's Next?

Concerning the times and the seasons, brethren, you have no need that I should write to you. For you yourselves know perfectly that the day of the Lord so comes as a thief in the night.

1 Thessalonians 5:1-2

What's next on the world scene? What can we expect to read in the headlines tomorrow? What will the coming year hold?

There are many possibilities, but one stands out above all others: the imminent and sudden appearing of Jesus Christ. The Bible tells us to be watchful and ready for His return, which could happen at any moment.

Apart from that, I wouldn't be surprised to see some of the following scenarios play out as I speculate about what will be next. While none of these *has to happen* before Jesus makes His appearance, any of them *could happen*.

1. A Rush Toward a Worldwide Economic Solution

The world is in economic turmoil, with nations increasingly in debt and financial instability looming large. There could be a push for a global economic solution, perhaps a unified currency or economic system, to address these challenges. This aligns with the prophetic vision of a one-world economy found in Revelation 13:16-17.

2. An Aggressive Attempt to Reinstate Global Fear Tactics

We have seen how fear can be used to control and manipulate people. Recent events hint at the potential for new waves of global fear tactics. Such measures could be used to gain greater control over populations, as we witnessed during the COVID panic.

3. The Destruction of Damascus

Bible scholars don't know where to place the prophecies of Isaiah 17:1 and Jeremiah 49:23-27, which describe the complete destruction of Damascus, stating that it will become a ruinous heap. Currently, Damascus is well-populated, but the Bible predicts a sudden and catastrophic event that will leave it desolate. Some believe this event could be a trigger for larger regional conflicts, potentially setting the stage for the Ezekiel 38 battle. No one knows for certain when or how its destruction will play out, but I wouldn't be surprised if Damascus popped up in tomorrow's newsfeed.

4. A Russian-Led Islamic Coalition to Destroy Israel

Ezekiel 38-39 describes a coalition of nations led by Russia and Islamic countries that will come against Israel. This prophecy speaks of a future invasion that God Himself will intervene to stop. Given the current geopolitical alliances and tensions, this scenario seems increasingly plausible in the immediate future.

5. Increased Global Destabilization of Laws, Rule, and Order

We are witnessing a breakdown of law and order worldwide. There is a growing sense of chaos and destabilization in many countries, leading to societal unrest and upheaval. This aligns with the biblical description of the Last Days being marked by lawlessness and disorder (2 Thessalonians 2:7-8).

6. The Collapse of Europe as We Know It

The European Union faces numerous challenges, from economic crises to political fragmentation and social unrest. In short, Europe is hanging on by a thread, and its collapse could have significant global repercussions, affecting international relations and economies. Such an event would fit within the broader pattern of global instability prophesied in Scripture.

Or the Imminent and Sudden Appearing of Jesus Christ!

My hope is that the next world event to occur is the Rapture. This is our ultimate desire and what we should be rooting for above all else. Jesus promised that He would come again to take us to be with Him (John 14:3). The anticipation of His return should fill us with joy and motivate us to live faithfully and expectantly.

What happens next? I don't know. But I know the One who does, and that fills me with a comfort, a joy, and an anticipation of the day when we will be together with Him.

Questions for Thought or Discussion

Living with Expectation

How should the imminent return of Jesus Christ influence your daily life and decisions? What steps can you take to live more expectantly and faithfully?

Recognizing the Signs

Which of the potential global events mentioned resonates in your mind? Can you see the possibility of any of these things happening soon?

Staying Grounded

In a world full of uncertainty and fear, how can you stay grounded in your faith? What Scriptures or practices help you maintain peace and confidence in God's plan?

Let's Pray

Heavenly Father,

We see turmoil and uncertainty all around us, but we look to You and Your promises. Help us to live with the expectation of Jesus' imminent return, finding hope and strength in patient expectation. Give us wisdom to discern the times and courage to stand firm in our faith. May we be lights in the darkness, pointing others to the hope we have in Jesus Christ.

In Jesus' name we pray. Amen.

Day 12

Wars and Rumors of Wars

"You will hear of wars and rumors of wars. See that you are not troubled; for all these things must come to pass, but the end is not yet."

Matthew 24:6

One of the signs of the times that Jesus said we should be watching for is wars and rumors of wars. The Bible says there have always been wars because of our sinful desires: "Where do wars and fights come from among you? Do they not come from your desires for pleasure that war in your members? You lust and do not have. You murder and covet and cannot obtain. You fight and war" (James 4:1-2). But in the context of Matthew 24, Jesus is talking about wars on a global scale.

World War I ended in 1918, and people thought it was the war to end all wars because it was so horrific. Yet, Europe was back at it in the late 1930s and 40s. Today, many people believe that a third world war has already started, just in a different form. It's not always about blowing things up; sometimes it's about doing damage to economies and governments and public safety through more subtle or virtual means.

Jesus said that we should not be troubled but should expect these things. It should come as no surprise when the news headlines point to more and more conflict. Extreme tensions and outright conflicts persist around the globe. We see a constant stream of news highlighting these global tensions. In these days of globalism, why do we continue to see such conflicts?

Historically, we have seen that war can boost a struggling economy, and nations have actually engineered wars as a solution for distressed economic systems. Hitler stirred up war in Europe to boost Germany's failing economy. Some modern conflicts can be traced back to economic motivations as well.

Jesus warned us that days of war and warmongering would come. These global conflicts are not random; they fulfill His prophecy as a sign of the Last Days.

As believers, we need to recognize the signs of the times, but we needn't fear. Jesus said, "Let not your heart be troubled; you believe in God, believe also in Me. In My Father's house are many mansions; if it were not so, I would have told you. I go to prepare a place for you" (John 14:1-2). Jesus forewarned us about these events so we could remain vigilant and prepared. In a world riddled with conflict, our faith must remain anchored in Jesus, trusting in His sovereignty over history.

Don't panic when you read the headlines; instead look up.

Questions for Thought or Discussion

Understanding Prophecy

Have you noticed an increase in wars and rumors of wars in today's news? What does this tell us about the times we are living in?

Biblical Peace

How can you remain at peace and not be troubled by the global conflicts around you? What biblical promises can you hold onto for assurance?

Practical Faith

In what ways can you actively live out your faith and share the hope of the gospel in a world increasingly defined by conflict and uncertainty?

Let's Pray

Heavenly Father,

In these days of global turmoil and uncertainty, help us to trust in Your sovereign plan. Give us peace that surpasses understanding, and the courage to stand firm in our faith. Remind us that despite the chaos around us, Your Word remains true, and Your promises are unshakeable.

In Jesus' name we pray. Amen.

Countermeasures

> "Who then is a faithful and wise servant, whom his master made ruler over his household, to give them food in due season? Blessed is that servant whom his master, when he comes, will find so doing."
> MATTHEW 24:45-46

The times are turbulent, and as we watch and wait for the coming of Jesus, the opposition to our faith grows more hostile each day. In these unprecedented days, it's crucial to be equipped with biblical countermeasures against the enemy's schemes.

God's Word provides us with the tools we need to stay steadfast and victorious. Here are six countermeasures to help us meet the challenges we face:

Countermeasure #1: Have the Right Attitude

Intentionally and deliberately decide to think biblical thoughts. Matthew 24:45-50 highlights the importance of maintaining the right attitude. A faithful servant is one who remains diligent and wise, regardless of the uncertainty of the master's return. We must commit to aligning our thoughts with Scripture, not our emotions or circumstances. When our mindset is grounded in God's truth, we can respond to challenges with faith and obedience to Him.

Countermeasure #2: Keep Yourself Ready

Fellowship with other biblically minded Christ-followers. 2 Peter 2:1 warns us about false prophets and teachers who introduce destructive heresies. To stay ready, we must surround ourselves with fellow believers who encourage us and hold us accountable. Regular fellowship and discipleship help keep our faith sharp and our spirits prepared for Christ's return.

Countermeasure #3: Avoid Compromising Situations

Do not violate your conscience or the Scriptures. 1 Corinthians 10:31 reminds us to do everything for the glory of God. This means avoiding situations that tempt us to compromise our values and beliefs. Whether it's through media, relationships, or business dealings, we must guard our hearts and actions, ensuring they align with God's Word.

Countermeasure #4: Resist Complacency and Spiritual Laziness

Fight the temptation to "take a day off" from following Jesus. 2 Peter 3:3-5 speaks of scoffers in the Last Days, questioning the promise of His coming.

Spiritual complacency can creep in when we lose sight of Christ's imminent return. We must remain vigilant, continuously growing in our faith and resisting the urge to become spiritually lazy. Daily time in the Word and prayer are essential in maintaining our spiritual fervor.

Countermeasure #5: Exercise Extreme Judgment Regarding Information

Believe nothing you hear or see until it is proven. 1 Thessalonians 5:21-22 advises us to test all things and hold fast to what is good. In an age of misinformation and deception, it's crucial to scrutinize everything against the truth of Scripture. Whether it's news, teachings, or opinions, we must evaluate them critically and biblically to avoid being led astray.

Countermeasure #6: Galvanize Yourself with the Bible

Get so well-disciplined that the Bible becomes your first response. 2 Peter 1:5-8 calls us to add to our faith virtue, knowledge, self-control, perseverance, godliness, brotherly kindness, and love. By immersing ourselves in the Word of God, we become spiritually fortified, like galvanized steel resistant to the elements. This spiritual discipline ensures that when trials and temptations come, our default reaction is rooted in biblical truth.

Questions for Thought or Discussion

Attitude Check

How can you ensure that your thoughts are aligned with Scripture, especially in challenging situations?

Staying Ready

Regular fellowship with other believers strengthens your faith and preparedness for Christ's return. Give an example of how such community has impacted your spiritual growth.

Avoiding Compromise

Reflect on a situation where you were tempted to compromise your values. How did you handle it, and what did you learn from that experience?

Resisting Complacency

What are some practical steps you can take to avoid spiritual laziness? How do you stay motivated in your walk with Christ?

Evaluating Information

Discuss a recent piece of information you heard that needed to be validated against Scripture.

Galvanizing with the Bible

In what ways has immersing yourself in Scripture changed your responses to life's challenges? Give testimony to how the Bible has fortified your faith.

Let's Pray

Heavenly Father,

In these challenging times, help us to remain steadfast—watching and waiting. Guide us to have the right attitude, rooted in Your Word. Surround us with fellow believers who will encourage and sharpen us. Give us wisdom to avoid compromising situations and the strength to resist complacency. Help us to exercise discernment in all we hear and see, testing everything against Your truth. May we be galvanized by Your Word, strong and immovable in our faith. Thank You for Your guidance and protection.

In Jesus' name we pray. Amen.

Day 14

Why Jesus Tells Us the Future

"Now I have told you before it comes, that when it does come to pass, you may believe."

John 14:29

Why does the Bible contain prophecy? Why does God tell us what will happen in the future? Because He wants us to have assurance and confidence in Him.

We live in a world where unexpected events can cause fear and anxiety, but as believers, we have the assurance that God knows the future and has revealed it to us in His Word.

Here are three powerful statements made by Jesus to provide us with a foundation for our faith, ensuring we can face tomorrow with confidence:

1. "I tell you before it comes, that when it does come to pass, you may believe that I am He." John 13:19

Prophecy is a powerful tool for building faith. By revealing events before they happen, Jesus strengthens our trust in Him. He wants us to know that He is in control, and nothing takes Him by surprise. This foreknowledge is not just for information but for our transformation. When we see prophecies fulfilled, our belief in Jesus is reinforced, and we know that He is truly the Son of God.

Imagine a contractor building your house, or a doctor operating on you, or the pilot of your plane saying, "Uh-oh. I wasn't prepared for this. I never thought this type of complication could happen. I don't have procedures in place for this type of occurrence."

The anxiety and uncertainty you would feel would be immense! But Jesus is not like that. He provides us with certainty. He tells us in advance what will happen so that when it does, our faith is affirmed. We can rest assured that our Savior knows the future and is guiding us through it.

2. "Now I have told you before it comes, that when it does come to pass, you may believe." John 14:29

Here, Jesus repeats the assurance given in John 13:19. This repetition is crucial because it underscores the importance of prophecy in building our faith. Jesus knows that in our human frailty, we need constant reminders of His sovereignty and foreknowledge. By telling us what will happen before it does, He provides a foundation upon which to build our trust.

It's like having a detailed plan laid out before going on a road trip, or better yet, a tour guide, someone telling you exactly what will happen during your travels, including any challenges and how to overcome them. That would give you great confidence, wouldn't it? In the same way, Jesus' prophecies provide us with a roadmap for the future, ensuring that when we face trials, we can recall His words and find comfort and strength.

3. "These things I have told you, that when the time comes, you may remember that I told you of them." John 16:4

Jesus emphasizes the importance of remembering His words. When the foretold events occur, recalling His predictions brings comfort and fortifies our faith. Knowing that Jesus has already seen and told us about the future assures us that He is in control. This remembrance acts as a source of peace amid chaos.

Revelation 19:10 tells us that "the testimony of Jesus is the spirit of prophecy." The prophecy that we read in the Bible is a testimony to Jesus' divinity and truth. The purpose of prophecy is not merely to predict the future but to testify about Jesus and His power. It assures us that Jesus is who He says He is and that we can trust Him with our past, present, and future.

The Bible is filled with prophecies that have been fulfilled and those yet to come. This prophetic foundation builds our faith and gives us the confidence to face the unknown—because it's not unknown to Him.

Questions for Thought or Discussion

Prophecy's Purpose

Why do you think God uses prophecy to reveal future events? How does knowing the future, as revealed in the Bible, impact your faith and trust in God?

The Road Ahead

Are you into maps? Does having a "roadmap" from Jesus about the End Times give you a greater sense of confidence as you travel life's road?

Jesus' Testimony

Revelation 19:10 says that "the testimony of Jesus is the spirit of prophecy." How does the fulfillment of biblical prophecy testify to Jesus' divinity and truth?

Let's Pray

Heavenly Father,

Thank You for the assurance Your Word provides. We are grateful for the prophecies that build our faith and the reminders of Your sovereignty. Help us to remember Your words and find comfort in Your promises. Thank you that we can face the future with confidence, knowing that You are in control and have prepared the way for us. Strengthen our faith and help us to trust in You completely.

In Jesus' name we pray. Amen.

Day 15

Hope for the Future

This hope we have as an anchor of the soul, both sure and steadfast.

Hebrews 6:19

Faith and hope are intricately connected. Faith is the foundation, and hope is the structure built upon it. When God makes a promise, prophecy, or prediction, our faith in His Word naturally leads us to hope for its fulfillment. As believers, our hope is anchored in the certainty of God's promises.

"God said it. I believe it. That settles it." This old saying captures the essence of faith. However, if we truly believe what God has said, it will be evident in our lives through hope. Hope is the visible sign of our faith in action.

Hope Is an Internal Rudder

Hope acts as an internal rudder, guiding us in our decision-making and helping us navigate life's uncertainties. The Bible tells us in Ecclesiastes 3:11 that God has placed eternity in our hearts. The innate desire for something beyond this life drives our hope. Hope is not a fleeting emotion but a steadfast anchor for our souls, enabling us to make wise choices and avoid hasty decisions.

Hope Is an External Message

Hope is not just for internal guidance; it is also an external message to the world. Our lives should radiate hope, especially in challenging times. This external hope is a testimony to those around us that showcases the strength and assurance we have in Christ.

Hope Is a Projected Strength

In the midst of chaos and uncertainty, when life's challenges hit hard—when the "bombs are bursting in air" and everything seems to be falling apart—our steadfast hope in Jesus stands out. Hope that is settled in Christ becomes evident to those around us in times of difficulty.

Your friends, neighbors, and family will look to see how you deal with adversity. They will observe your reactions and draw strength from your calm assurance. Because your hope is anchored in Christ, you can face difficult days with confidence. This hope is not of your own making; it is Christ's strength shining through you.

As believers, we cannot separate the future from hope. "'For I know the plans I have for you,' declares the Lord, 'plans to prosper you and not to harm you, plans to give you hope and a future'" (Jeremiah 29:11).

Our hope is anchored in the certainty of God's Word. Let this hope guide us internally, shine through us externally, and project strength to those around us. In doing so, we fulfill our calling as bearers of the hope found in Christ.

Questions for Thought or Discussion

Internal Rudder

How can you allow hope to act as an internal rudder, guiding your decisions and actions in your faith journey? Reflect on a time when hope in God's promises helped you navigate a challenging situation.

External Message

How does your life currently reflect the external message of hope to others? What are some practical ways you can demonstrate this hope to your friends, neighbors, and family?

Projected Strength

In what ways can your hope in Christ serve as a projected strength during difficult times? Is a calm assurance in Jesus visible to those around you when they need it most?

Let's Pray

Heavenly Father,

Thank You for the hope we have in You, anchored in Your promises. Guide our decisions through the lens of hope and help us deliver the message of hope to those around us. In challenging times, let Your strength shine through us, revealing the assurance we have in Christ.

In Jesus' name we pray. Amen.

Day 16

Jesus Is Coming!

The Lord Himself will descend from heaven with a shout, with the voice of an archangel, and with the trumpet of God. And the dead in Christ will rise first. Then we who are alive and remain shall be caught up together with them in the clouds to meet the Lord in the air. And thus we shall always be with the Lord.

1 Thessalonians 4:16-17

The Rapture is the event in which Jesus Christ will return to collect His believers in the air, the physical bodies of those living and deceased, and take them to heaven. It will happen suddenly and without warning. Though it can fall under the umbrella of the Second Coming, the Rapture is separate from Christ's physical return to Jerusalem. The Rapture is promised to us by none other than Jesus Christ Himself in John 14:1-3:

> "Let not your heart be troubled; you believe in God, believe also in Me. In My Father's house are many mansions; if it were not so,

> I would have told you. I go to prepare a place for you. And if I go and prepare a place for you, I will come again and receive you to Myself; that where I am, there you may be also."

Jesus very clearly tells us that He's coming to get us and will bring us to the place He has prepared for us.

How do we get there? What is the vehicle? The Rapture. We will be "caught up," off of this globe and out of this world. He will collect both the living and the dead who are His in the atmosphere. And from there, He will take us into His presence in heaven, away from all that will happen on earth. That is thrilling news.

Jesus promises to descend from heaven, raise the dead in Christ, and catch us up together with Him in the air. And then He promises that we shall always be with Him. That's a promise worth placing your hope and trust in.

The Rapture will be sudden. There are no prophetic precursors or requirements for it to take place. It is imminent, and it will be without warning. There are no unfulfilled prophecies standing in the way of it. Jesus is coming! Are you ready?

The Rapture will happen in the twinkling of an eye. It's a sudden event. We read in 1 Corinthians 15:51-52:

> Behold, I tell you a mystery: We shall not all sleep, but we shall all be changed—in a moment, in the twinkling of an eye,

at the last trumpet. For the trumpet will sound, and the dead will be raised incorruptible, and we shall be changed.

How long will it take for us to be changed? "In the twinkling of an eye." Experts argue whether that's 18 thousandths of a second or 22 thousandths of a second. Who cares? It's fast!

The dead will be raised incorruptible (not as decaying zombies from a horror film, but incorruptible—not capable of deteriorating), and we, the saints who are still alive, shall be transformed, metamorphosed, molecularly transfigured. Isn't that amazing to think about?

God's Word is certain. Don't let anyone tell you otherwise. God will fulfill His prophetic Word. He always has. And what's left for Him to fulfill, He will do. You can count on Him.

Jesus could come back this year, this month, or even this very day. I pray He comes soon. And until that day, I encourage you to stay in the Word of God, watching, waiting, and working to bring others to Him in these remarkable days.

Questions for Thought or Discussion

The Promise of the Rapture

How does the promise of the Rapture provide comfort and hope for you? What aspects of Jesus' promise in John 14:1-3 resonate most deeply with you?

Living in Expectation

What does it mean to live in a state of readiness for Jesus' imminent return? Are there changes you might need to make in your life in light of the Rapture?

Encouraging Others

Have you ever shared the hope of the Rapture with someone who may not be aware of this promise? Have you ever encouraged and comforted other believers with the words of this promise?

Let's Pray

Heavenly Father,

Thank You for the promise of the Rapture and the assurance that Jesus will return to take us to the place He has prepared. Help us to live in a state of readiness, always watching and waiting for His return. Strengthen our faith and give us the courage to share this hope with others. May we remain faithful and diligent in our walk with You, knowing that Your Word is true, and Your promises are sure.

In Jesus' name we pray. Amen.

Day 17

Who Will Be Raptured?

I do not want you to be ignorant, brethren, concerning those who have fallen asleep, lest you sorrow as others who have no hope. For if we believe that Jesus died and rose again, even so God will bring with Him those who sleep in Jesus. For this we say to you by the word of the Lord, that we who are alive and remain until the coming of the Lord will by no means precede those who are asleep.

1 Thessalonians 4:13-15

Who's involved in the Rapture? The answer is simple: the dead in Christ and the living in Christ.

The Believing Dead

The first group involved in the Rapture is those who have died in Christ. Their spirits are already in the presence of Jesus, but their bodies remain here on earth, awaiting resurrection. At the moment of the Rapture, their bodies will be resurrected and transformed, reuniting with their spirits in an instant.

Think about it this way: if you were to die right now, your body would fall to the ground, but your spirit would immediately be with Jesus. Your body might be buried, cremated, or lost at sea, but that doesn't matter to God. He knows where every particle of your physical being is, and He will raise and transform it.

The Living Believers

The second group involved in the Rapture is those Christians who are alive at the time of Jesus' return. These believers will be caught up with the resurrected dead to meet Jesus in the air. This will happen in the twinkling of an eye. The living believers will be instantly transformed, their mortal bodies changed into glorified bodies fit for eternity.

All of Nature Groans

We live in a world full of grief and suffering, evidence of the fall of mankind. We see sickness, death, and injustice all around us, affecting humans, animals, and the entire planet. The Bible tells us in Romans 8:22 that "the whole creation groans and labors with birth pangs together until now."

As believers, we grieve, but not as those who have no hope. We all walk in a fog of grief, whether it's seeing someone suffering from sickness, the loss of a loved one, or witnessing brutality in nature like a gazelle being taken by a lion. Our hearts wrench when we see children born with defects or when we witness the many other injustices in the world. This grief is a reminder that this world is not our home, and that Jesus has promised to take us away from all of this.

In the book of Romans, Paul tells us that we "groan within ourselves, eagerly waiting for the adoption, the redemption of our body" (Romans 8:23). This groaning is a longing for the Rapture, when our bodies will be made new. The suffering and decay we see around us remind us that this is not the end. There is a glorious future awaiting us.

United in Christ

The Rapture will unite all believers—past and present—into one glorious assembly. The Church, made up of people from every tribe, tongue, and nation, will be gathered together to meet the Lord in the air. This diverse and beautiful body of believers is the Bride of Christ, loved and cherished by Him.

Black, white, and every color in between; from every social, economic, and cultural background; from every continent and nationality—whatever our pigmentation or language, every tribe and nation is represented. Jesus says, "That's My Church. Isn't she beautiful?" He loves us and He cherishes His unified Church.

The Church is not just a building or a local congregation; it's the global body of Christ followers—living and dead. We are united in our faith in Jesus, and this unity will be fully realized at the Rapture.

Questions for Thought or Discussion

Expectation and Reunion

Do you know a believer who has died? How does the promise of reuniting with them in the air make you feel?

Unity in Christ

What does it mean to you to be part of a global Church that will one day be united with Christ in the Rapture?

Hope Amidst Groaning

Does the hope of Jesus' imminent return help temper the sadness caused by the reality of suffering in this world?

Let's Pray

Heavenly Father,

Thank You for the promise of the Rapture and the assurance that Jesus will come again to take us to be with Him and with those who have gone before us. Strengthen our faith as we navigate the grief and suffering of this world, knowing that You have a perfect plan for our future. Unite us as Your Church, diverse yet one in Christ, and help us to live in a way that honors You until the day You call us home.

In Jesus' name we pray. Amen.

Day 18

Bible Prophecy Matters

I have not shunned to declare to you the whole counsel of God.

Acts 20:27

Many individuals have come from churches or denominations that never touch the topic of Bible prophecy. People from these places often know very little about the book of Revelation or the End Times events mentioned in Ezekiel or Daniel. On the other side of the spectrum are people who have been taught all kinds of crazy things about Bible prophecy and their doctrine of the Last Days is unscriptural.

Listen, it's crucial that we as believers know and understand the whole counsel of God. From Genesis to Revelation, it's all important. Those preachers and teachers who never touch on the subject of prophecy because they don't understand it, or are afraid they can't answer questions that arise, or believe that it's all symbolic and allegorical, these people are doing their church members a grave disservice.

I had a realization the other day while driving. I stopped at a red light and saw a really cool flatbed transporter truck. On the back was a beautiful red Ferrari. As I admired the Ferrari, I couldn't help but wonder why it was on the back of a truck. For all I knew, it could have been missing an entire engine; there was no way I could tell.

Then it hit me: churches can be like that. They may look impressive on the outside, with extensive facilities, jaw-dropping architecture, beautiful stained glass, and great worship services, but there's something missing. They're like that Ferrari on the truck; they look like they should be moving forward at impressive speeds, but they're not.

If someone offered you a ride in a Ferrari, you'd probably say yes without hesitation. But as soon as you found out that the Ferrari had no engine and was strapped to the back of a transporter truck going 40 miles per hour, you'd have a different response. It just wouldn't be the same experience.

In the same way, the doctrine of Christ's imminent return cannot be missing from your theology. Why? Because when you believe Jesus Christ is coming back soon and can call His Church home in an instant, your faith will be more alive and active. When you understand that the people you know will go through a time of extreme tribulation if they don't have Christ, you'll be motivated to tell them about Him. When you understand the whole counsel of God, you'll be striving to live fully for Him, not just going through the motions.

I don't care how nice a church looks or how great the music is. What matters is whether it is teaching the full truth of God's Word. If you're feeling uncomfortable with the idea of Jesus coming back, maybe it's time to accept Him as your Savior. When you do, He'll ignite your faith and empower you to live for Him.

Questions for Thought or Discussion

The Whole Counsel of God

Acts 20:27 emphasizes the importance of knowing and declaring the whole counsel of God. Why do you think some churches or denominations avoid teaching on Bible prophecy? How can a lack of understanding in this area affect believers?

Balancing Understanding

Consider the spectrum mentioned in the devotion, from churches that neglect Bible prophecy to those that teach unscriptural interpretations. How can we be sure to understand Bible prophecy while avoiding extremes or misinterpretations?

Christ's Imminent Return

How does the metaphor of the Ferrari on the truck illustrate the importance of including End Times doctrine in your theology? How does believing in Jesus' imminent return impact your faith and actions?

Let's Pray

Heavenly Father,

Thank You for the revelation of Your Word, which contains the whole counsel of God. Help us to embrace and understand every aspect of Your truth, including Bible prophecy. Give us discernment to navigate teachings and interpretations, guiding us to the truth revealed in Scripture. Ignite within us a fervent expectation of Christ's imminent return, empowering us to live faithfully and fully for Him each day. We want our lives to reflect both the hope and the joy found in knowing that Jesus is coming back soon.

In Jesus' name we pray. Amen.

Day 19

Six Reasons for Studying Bible Prophecy

I do not want you to be ignorant, brethren, concerning those who have fallen asleep, lest you sorrow as others who have no hope.
1 Thessalonians 4:13

Studying Bible prophecy is not just so we know what will happen. It's a spiritual exercise that leads to greater intimacy with God and rewards from Him. As Jeremiah 29:12-13 assures us, "Then you will call upon Me and go and pray to Me, and I will listen to you. And you will seek Me and find Me, when you search for Me with all your heart." This diligent search for God through His prophetic Word invites His presence and blessing into our lives.

Hebrews 11:6 reminds us that "without faith it is impossible to please Him, for he who comes to God must believe that He is, and that He is a rewarder of those who diligently seek Him." When we earnestly study prophecy in faith, we please God and open ourselves to His rewards.

Why should we study Bible prophecy? Here are six good reasons:

1. Resilience Against Temptation

When you immerse yourself in God's Word, including prophetic books like Revelation and Daniel, you will find yourself developing a supernatural resilience against the temptations of this world. Just as food fuels your body and gas powers your car, understanding the entirety of God's Word will galvanize you against worldly temptations. You can trust in God's promises, and this trust will make you resilient.

2. Increased Endurance

Studying Bible prophecy equips you with the strength to endure life's challenges. When you understand that this world is not your permanent home, you gain a biblical perspective that helps you endure difficulties. Recognizing that there is an end—and a new beginning—on the horizon gives you the strength to persevere, knowing that God keeps His promises.

3. Diminished Sinful Habits and Thoughts

The more you focus on Christ's return, the weaker sinful habits and thoughts become in your life. This is called holiness: God working in you, not through your own efforts but through His transforming power. As you focus on the reality of Christ's return, you will notice that the grip of sin diminishes, and you will grow in righteousness.

4. Heavenly Perspective

With a focus on Bible prophecy, you will find yourself thinking, speaking, and acting with a heavenly perspective. You will become excited about doing things that bless God's heart. True revival happens within people who are deeply engaged with God's Word; they start living out its truth, which impacts their daily lives as well as those around them.

5. Desire to Serve and Love Others

Immersing yourself in Scripture naturally leads to a desire to serve and love others. As the Bible works within you, it stirs you up, giving you renewed spiritual energy. You'll find yourself asking, "How can I serve? What can I do?" This transformation moves you from being a passive observer to an active participant in God's work.

6. High View of Scripture

Studying Bible prophecy helps you develop a profound respect and love for Scripture. It becomes more than just a Sunday obligation; it's a daily source of life and guidance. The Bible comes alive, and you start valuing it deeply, recognizing its relevance and authority in every aspect of your life.

We must embrace the full counsel of God's Word, including prophecy, allowing it to transform our lives and deepen our faith. With each insight and revelation, may we draw closer to God, stand firm against the world's opposition, and eagerly await the return of our Lord Jesus Christ.

Questions for Thought or Discussion

Resilience in Temptation
How has your understanding of Bible prophecy strengthened your resilience to temptation and worldly pressures?

Endurance in Trials
Reflect on a specific instance where focusing on biblical prophecy helped you endure a challenging situation. How did this perspective shape your response and outlook?

Impact on Daily Life
Would you say you have a heavenly perspective in your thoughts, speech, and actions. How should studying Bible prophecy influence your daily decisions and interactions with others?

Let's Pray

Heavenly Father,

Thank You for the treasure of Your Word, which reveals Your plans and promises for the future. As we study Bible prophecy, we ask for Your guidance and illumination. May each reason for studying prophecy become a reality in our lives, transforming us into faithful disciples who live with hope and purpose. Empower us to serve and love others, reflecting Your character to the world. May our reverence for Your Word deepen as we continue to prayerfully read, study, and memorize it.

In Jesus' name we pray. Amen.

Day 20

Setting the Scene

Let no one deceive you by any means; for that Day will not come unless the falling away comes first, and the man of sin is revealed, the son of perdition.

2 Thessalonians 2:3

Have you ever attended a play and experienced the transition between scenes? The stage goes dark, and a black mesh screen drops, obscuring your view. You can see just enough movement behind the screen to pique your curiosity, but the details remain hidden until the lights come back on, and the new scene is revealed. That behind-the-scenes activity is essential for setting the stage for what comes next. Similarly, our world is experiencing a behind-the-scenes preparation for a major prophetic event: the rise of the Antichrist.

An eye-opening statement by former Belgian Prime Minister Paul-Henri Spaak highlights this anticipation: "We do not want another committee. We have too many already. What we want is a man of sufficient stature to hold the allegiance of all people and to lift us out of the economic morass into which we are sinking. Send us such a man and be he god or devil, we will receive him."

This sentiment reflects a growing desire for a powerful leader who can provide solutions to global crises. After the Rapture, when believers are taken to be with the Lord, the world will be left in chaos. This post-Rapture world, described in 2 Thessalonians 2:3, will be marked by the revelation of the "man of sin," also known as the Antichrist. Matthew 24:21 warns that this will be a time of unprecedented tribulation, a period unlike any other in history. Deception will become rampant, and those who rejected the truth will be given over to a strong delusion, believing the lies of the lawless one.

A Cry for Peace and Safety

In the aftermath of the Rapture, there will be a desperate cry for peace and safety. 1 Thessalonians 5:1-3 explains that while the people seek peace, sudden destruction will come upon them, similar to labor pains upon a pregnant woman, and they will not escape. The Antichrist will rise to power by promising peace and stability, using deception to gain control. Daniel 8:25 reveals that through his policies and seductive calm, the Antichrist will destroy many, magnifying himself and causing deception to prosper.

Deception and Delusion

Deception will become the norm in this post-Rapture world. 2 Thessalonians 2:9-11 describes the coming of the lawless one, empowered by Satan, performing signs and wonders to deceive those who have rejected the truth.

A World in Freefall

The post-Rapture world will be characterized by unprecedented chaos and instability. As societies and governments struggle to maintain order, the Antichrist will present himself as the savior who can restore peace and stability. However, this peace will be deceptive, masking the true intentions of the lawless one. The Antichrist will usher in a period of great tribulation, where he will demand worship and allegiance, further leading humanity into spiritual darkness.

A Global Economic Reset

Revelation 13:16-17 speaks of a global economic system where the Antichrist will cause all people to receive a mark on their right hand or forehead, without which no one can buy or sell. This economic reset will create a unified system of control, further solidifying the Antichrist's power over the world.

Satan's Man in the Shadows

Satan is always preparing for the End Times by keeping a potential Antichrist figure in the shadows, ready to step into the spotlight. This preparation is ongoing because Satan does not know the exact timing of the end. Throughout history, he has had various candidates lined up, waiting for the moment to reveal his chosen one. This constant state of readiness emphasizes the reality of the spiritual battle we're engaged in.

Questions for Thought or Discussion

Setting the Stage
How can you recognize the behind-the-scenes preparations in the world today that point to the fulfillment of Bible prophecy?

Resilience in Deception
Are you allowing yourself to be deceived? What are you reading? What are you listening to? Where do you get your worldview opinions?

Seeking Truth
Reflect on the importance of seeking and loving the truth of God's Word. How can this commitment protect you from the delusions described in the Scriptures?

Let's Pray

Heavenly Father,

Thank You for revealing Your plans and purposes through Your Word. As we witness the world setting the stage for future events, help us to remain steadfast in our faith and discerning of the times. Guard our hearts against deception and strengthen our commitment to seek and uphold Your truth.

In Jesus' name we pray. Amen.

Day 21

Getting Ready for the Big Day

As He who called you is holy, you also be holy in all your conduct, because it is written, "Be holy, for I am holy."
1 Peter 1:15-16

The phrase "getting ready for the big day" conjures up vivid images for each of us. Perhaps we think of a graduation, or a wedding, or moving into a new house. In a way, all those things point to the biggest day of all: the day we will finally get to be with Jesus.

In Southern California where I live, we typically have about 20 days a year with cloud cover or rain. Most days are beautiful, even in the winter, when temperatures can still easily be in the high 70s. But even for us Southern Californians, as parents, we do everything necessary to ensure that before our children go out to enjoy the day, they are properly dressed for the conditions—whether that is bundled up in layers or slathered in sunscreen—for their protection, comfort, and safety.

Depending on where you live, you dress according to your local weather, some in thick parkas and snowshoes, others in flip-flops and board shorts. You dress for the occasion, prepared for the atmosphere, and you ensure your children do the same, getting them ready for what they will encounter and experience.

Similarly, God is getting us ready for heaven. He is dressing us in spiritual attire to develop our walk with Him. As we prepare for the big day, let's explore a few key verses.

Pursue Peace and Holiness

Hebrews 12:14 instructs us: "Pursue peace with all people, and holiness, without which no one will see the Lord." We are to strive to live at peace with everyone and to be holy. Holiness means being set apart for God's purposes, dedicated to Him. It's not about being sinless or perfect, but about being devoted to God. Without this dedication, it is impossible to see the Lord.

Be Holy in All Conduct

1 Peter 1:15-16 says, "As He who called you is holy, you also be holy in all your conduct, because it is written, 'Be holy, for I am holy.'" Again, holiness is not about being perfect. None of us can do that. Holiness means being solely devoted to God, surrendering our lives to Him. It involves yielding to His will and letting Him shape our lives. This call to holiness is about living in a way that reflects God's character.

Love and Obedience

In John 14:15, Jesus said, "If you love Me, keep My commandments." His commandments boil down to loving God and loving one another. The beauty of these commands is that God doesn't expect us to fulfill them through our own efforts. He asks us to surrender to Him, allowing Him to establish these truths in our lives through the power of the Holy Spirit.

It's liberating to know that we don't have to strive in our own strength to accomplish these things. Whatever God invites you and me to do, He doesn't expect us to do them in the efforts of our flesh, in the efforts of our trying. He expects us to surrender to Him and to let Him establish these things in our lives. I've often said, "Don't *do* Christianity. You'll get hurt. Instead, let Christianity *be done* to you."

In Zechariah 4:6, the Lord says, "Not by might nor by power, but by My Spirit." The Holy Spirit takes the Word of God and applies it to our lives, guiding us and empowering us to live according to His will. After we study the Bible, the Holy Spirit reminds us of what we've learned and helps us put it into practice.

As we prepare for the big day, we are called to be open, willing, and set apart for what the Lord has for us. This means allowing the Holy Spirit to work in us and through us, transforming us and preparing us for eternity with Jesus.

Questions for Thought or Discussion

Preparation

How are you currently preparing for the big day: your ultimate union with Jesus?

Holiness

What does being holy mean, and how can you apply the command to be holy in your daily life?

Love in Action

Reflect on John 14:15. What are just a few examples of the commandments Jesus has given and expects His disciples to obey?

Let's Pray

Heavenly Father,

Thank You for preparing us for the big day when we will meet Jesus. Help us to pursue peace with everyone and to live dedicated to You. Empower us by Your Holy Spirit to love You and others as You have commanded. We surrender our lives to You, trusting that You will guide and transform us. May we be open and willing to follow Your leading each and every day.

In Jesus' name we pray. Amen.

Day 22

Living with Urgency

Let us consider one another in order to stir up love and good works, not forsaking the assembling of ourselves together, as is the manner of some, but exhorting one another, and so much the more as you see the Day approaching.

Hebrews 10:24-25

In 1 Thessalonians 1:4-10, Paul taught the people of Thessalonica two key doctrines during his brief stay with them. First, he assured them that their salvation is secure in the Messiah. Second, he emphasized the fact that Christ is coming back. These two truths are the ultimate motivation for believers to share the hope available in Christ with the world. We don't need a seminary degree or an extensive library to do this; we have the Word of God and the power of the Holy Spirit Hebrews 10:24-25 reinforces this message.

As believers, we are called to interact with one another, challenging and encouraging each other to love and to do good works.

Love and Good Works

Love is a verb; it requires action. We are to love one another and those around us. This means engaging in activities that demonstrate this love. We should be praying for people at hospitals, offering hope outside abortion clinics, helping a neighbor with their yard work, or any of the thousands of ways we can practically and tangibly demonstrate God's love to those around us. In the early Roman Empire, even Caesar acknowledged that Christians loved one another. Our actions should reflect this love in real and practical ways.

The Importance of Gathering Together

Hebrews 10:25 urges us not to forsake assembling together. Regular fellowship is crucial for mutual encouragement and spiritual growth. In today's world, many have abandoned this practice, but the Bible commands us to gather and exhort one another especially as we see the day of Christ's return approaching. The world around us desperately needs the love and activity of the Church. We are not a company or a corporation; we are the Church of the living God, called to love and bless others.

The Imminent Return of Christ

The imminent return of Jesus is a powerful motivator. Scripture teaches that Jesus could come back at any moment. This reality should drive us to live purposefully, sharing the message of salvation with as many people as possible. Do we still go to work or school? Of course. Do we raise our families and do our chores and live our daily lives? Absolutely. But while we continue with our daily responsibilities, we must always be ready to meet the Lord. We never know when our time on earth will end, and we must be prepared.

Living with Purpose

As believers, everything about our lives should reflect the urgency of Christ's return. Yes, we engage in activities and responsibilities that make up the hours and minutes of our lives, but our ultimate purpose is to tell others about Jesus. This readiness isn't just about waiting for the end; it's about living a life that honors God and impacts others.

Questions for Thought or Discussion

Security in Salvation

How does knowing your salvation is secure in Christ influence your daily life and interactions with others?

Active Love

What practical steps can you take to show love and good works in your community?

Fellowship

Do you prioritize gathering with other believers to encourage and be encouraged?

Let's Pray

Heavenly Father,

Thank You for the assurance of our salvation in Christ and the promise of His return. Help us to live each day with the urgency and purpose that these truths bring. Empower us by Your Holy Spirit to love others and engage in good works. Strengthen our commitment to gather with fellow believers, encouraging one another as we see the day of Christ's return approaching.

In Jesus' name we pray. Amen.

Day 23

Racism: a Sign of the Times

"Nation will rise against nation."
MATTHEW 24:7

When asked what the signs of His coming would be, among the things Jesus listed was an increase in racism. In Matthew 24:7, He said, "Nation will rise against nation." The word translated as *nation* in English is the word *ethnos* in Greek. It's where we get the word *ethnicity* or *ethnic* groups. Jesus said that *ethnos* will rise up warring against *ethnos*. One of the indicators of the Last Days is that ethnicities will divide from one another, and they will war against each other.

Not only is that happening, but the world that we live in is stoking the flames of racism. It's as though the culture is hell-bent on a course of destruction. That's because a culture without God is a destructive culture. It's amazing to me that the news media, print, radio, songs, movies—all of them—are stoking the angst: whites should hate blacks, blacks should hate Hispanics, and so on. It's remarkable.

Recently, I was getting ready to go to church, and I looked over at the bathtub. It was clear that my granddaughter had been there. How did I know? Because there were a bunch of toys left in it. What I saw there made me stop and think of Matthew 24:7.

Do you know what I saw in the bathtub? I saw teacups. I saw little chairs and little tables, and I saw little combs. And then, I saw a white Barbie, a brown Barbie, and a black Barbie—all of them were in the bathtub where they had obviously enjoyed a tea party together. That simple scene blessed my heart. I thought, *What's so cool about this is that my granddaughter has no knowledge that this one's white, that one is brown, and the other one is black.* It was awesome.

Jesus said in the Last Days, we will have indicators that the end is near, and one of those indicators will be ethnic groups warring against ethnic groups. You know why that's true? Because so many people don't have Jesus in their heart. When there's no Jesus in our hearts, we parse ourselves up, we divide, we get into little cliques and groups, and God hates that.

Go to the book of Revelation to see a picture of what heaven is like. The Bible says in heaven there are those from every kindred, tribe, tongue, and nation of the earth.

The world tries to divide us, emphasizing our differences and stirring up conflict. But in Christ, we are called to unity. In heaven, all people come together in perfect harmony, worshiping God as one. This unity reflects God's heart and His desire for His people to live in love and peace.

As believers, we must resist the world's push toward division and embrace the unity that Christ brings. We must love one another, regardless of our backgrounds, and foster peace among ethnicities. Jesus prayed for our unity as believers in John 17:21, saying, "[I pray] that they all may be one, as You, Father, are in Me, and I in You; that they also may be one in Us, that the world may believe that You sent Me."

Let's live out this unity as we watch and wait for the Lord's return, showing the world the love and peace of Christ. Let's break down the barriers that divide and build bridges of understanding and compassion. By doing so, we reflect the kingdom of God and offer a compelling witness to a world in desperate need of hope and healing.

Questions for Thought or Discussion

Increase in Racism
What current events give evidence to the fact that ethnic and racial division are on the rise?

Love in Action
What does it look like for you to show love to people from different ethnic backgrounds?

Combat the Division

How can you combat the negative influences of media that promote division?

Let's Pray

Heavenly Father,

We come before You with hearts open to Your love and guidance in this area. We ask for Your help in breaking down the barriers that divide us. Teach us to love one another as You have loved us. Help us to see past our differences and embrace the unity that You desire for us. May our actions reflect Your love and bring healing.

In Jesus' name we pray. Amen.

Day 24

The Judgments of the Tribulation

Then I heard a loud voice from the temple saying to the seven angels, "Go, pour out the seven bowls of God's wrath on the earth."

Revelation 16:1

In today's society, the call for social justice is louder than ever. People demand fairness and equity, wanting recompense for the wrongs they see in the world. They are quick to point out that our justice systems are broken and unfair.

That's because the God of the Bible is the only One who can exercise true and complete judgment and justice. He is the ultimate judge, and His judgments are perfect. While we seek justice on earth, we must remember that God's justice is unparalleled, and His full judgment is still to come.

What's ironic about our hypocritical age is everybody talks about justice and judgment, but when God shows His justice and judgment in the pages of Scripture, nobody wants to hear about it. When faced with the reality of God's justice, there is resistance and denial.

Nevertheless, the book of Revelation reveals the severity and certainty of God's judgment during the tribulation period. This judgment is necessary because God is just, fair, and holy.

The Recipients of God's Judgment

Who will face God's judgment during the Tribulation? The book of Revelation describes the recipients as those who have rejected God and lived in rebellion against Him. This judgment is not arbitrary; it is a necessary consequence of God's holiness and justice. The middle chapters of Revelation detail the horrific and gruesome judgments that will befall the earth. Here is a quick list.

The Judgments of Revelation

1. **The Seal Judgments (Revelation 6:1-17, 8:1-5)**

- The first seal: A conqueror comes in on a white horse.
- The second seal: War and conflict persist.
- The third seal: Famine and scarcity abound.
- The fourth seal: Death increases.
- The fifth seal: The martyrs' cry for justice.
- The sixth seal: Cosmic disturbances unfold.
- The seventh seal: There is silence in heaven and the trumpet judgments are introduced.

2. The Trumpet Judgments (Revelation 8:6-9:21, 11:15-19)

- The first trumpet: Hail and fire mixed with blood.
- The second trumpet: A burning mountain thrown into the sea.
- The third trumpet: A star called Wormwood falls, poisoning waters.
- The fourth trumpet: Darkness strikes the sky.
- The fifth trumpet: Demonic locusts torment humanity.
- The sixth trumpet: Four angels release a demonic army.
- The seventh trumpet: The temple of God in heaven is opened.

3. The Bowl Judgments (Revelation 16:1-21)

- The first bowl: Painful sores appear on those with the mark of the beast.
- The second bowl: The sea turns to blood.
- The third bowl: Rivers and springs turn to blood.
- The fourth bowl: Scorching heat radiates from the sun.
- The fifth bowl: Darkness and pain ensue.
- The sixth bowl: The Euphrates River dries up.
- The seventh bowl: A devastating earthquake and hailstorm occur.

The judgments of this time are so severe and horrific that Jesus said, "Then there will be great tribulation, such as has not been since the beginning of the world until this time, no, nor ever shall be. And unless those days were shortened, no flesh would be saved; but for the elect's sake those days will be shortened" (Matthew 24:21-22).

How Does This Apply to Us?

As believers, we look forward to the fact that we will be raptured before these judgments occur. So why should we concern ourselves with these future events?

The knowledge of what is to come should motivate us to witness to thel lost. Understanding the severity of God's judgment should stir us to share the hope and salvation found in Jesus Christ. We don't want anyone to experience the horrors described in Revelation.

This knowledge is a catalyst for evangelism. It compels us to reach out with urgency and compassion. We have a responsibility to warn others and guide them to the message of salvation.

Questions for Thought or Discussion

Divine Justice

How does the concept of God's perfect justice influence your views on human justice?

Revelation's Judgments

What emotions do you feel when you think about the seal, trumpet, and bowl judgments?

Motivated by Love

Does the knowledge of future judgment motivate you to share the gospel more fervently?

Let's Pray

Heavenly Father,

We acknowledge Your perfect justice and righteousness. As we think about the terrible judgments to come, help us internalize the urgency of sharing the gospel with those who do not know You. Fill us with compassion and boldness to be Your witnesses. May we be instruments of Your love in a world desperately in need of hope.

In Jesus' name we pray. Amen.

Day 25

For Such a Time as This

"If you remain completely silent at this time, relief and deliverance will arise for the Jews from another place, but you and your father's house will perish. Yet who knows whether you have come to the kingdom for such a time as this?"

Esther 4:14

When you think of the prophetic books in the Bible, Esther doesn't immediately spring to mind. But it is prophetic because it speaks to today's circumstances and gives us a model to follow as we encounter trouble in the Last Days.

The most well-known phrase from the book of Esther is "for such a time as this." This phrase was spoken by Mordecai to Esther when the Jewish people were facing extermination under the edict of the wicked man Haman. Mordecai urged Esther to approach the king and plead for her people, reminding her that her royal position might be part of God's plan to save the Jews. Mordecai called Esther to step into her divine purpose, risking her life to fulfill God's plan.

If you are a believer in Christ, you too have been brought into His kingdom for such a time as this. I know this for certain because God wastes nothing. He wastes not a moment, and certainly not your life. The fact of the matter is, no matter where you are or who you may be, you are living right now by the awesome decree of God, and it's His will that you are alive at this specific time.

God has appointed us to the same purpose as Esther, for such a time as this. We are not to be silent but to speak out against evil. The Hamans of this world are still threatening and opposing God's people, God's plan, God's purposes. You and I are here because we are living in a prophetic time. Jesus Christ is coming back soon, and we are to be busy about our Father's business, declaring the salvation that is found in Jesus. We're here now for a purpose.

God is on His throne in heaven, and His will is being lived out. We don't want to miss out on that. We want to be right in the middle of it. Whatever God's going to do next, let's be part of it. All that's happened in your life—the good, the bad, and the ugly—God uses it, and He redeems it. What a redemptive God. These Last Days' events include you. That should be a thrilling thought and cause you to pray, "God, how do You want to use me?"

Here's something to think about: God seems to show up most in times of trouble. Esther was in trouble.

Mordecai was in trouble. Daniel was in trouble. Noah was in trouble. Moses was in trouble. You want to see God show up in big ways? Get in trouble. I mean that in a good way. When we stand in the middle of God's will, trouble will come against us. But our God shows up in times of trouble!

Jeremiah 1:4-5 says, "The word of the Lord came to me, saying, 'Before I formed you in the womb, I knew you; before you were born I sanctified you; I ordained you a prophet to the nations.'" God was speaking to Jeremiah, but He could say the same thing to you and me. Before you were born, God sanctified you. It means He set you aside for a purpose. The God of the Bible, who gave you life and brought you into this world, has done so with a purpose.

You are here for such a time as this.

Questions for Thought or Discussion

Consider Your Calling
Do you believe that you are here for such a time as this? How does that belief shape your actions and decisions?

God's Sovereignty
How does knowing that God has a purpose for your life help you face challenges and uncertainties?

Purposeful Living
What steps can you take to ensure you are fulfilling God's purpose for you in the Last Days?

Let's Pray

Heavenly Father,

Thank You for reminding us that we are here for such a time as this. Help us to embrace Your purpose for our lives with courage and faith. Guide us to be bold witnesses for Christ, sharing the hope and salvation we have in Him. Use us mightily in these Last Days to bring glory to Your name.

In Jesus' name we pray. Amen.

Day 26

We Are Watchmen

Again the word of the L<small>ORD</small> came to me, saying, "Son of man, speak to the children of your people, and say to them: 'When I bring the sword upon a land, and the people of the land take a man from their territory and make him their watchman, when he sees the sword coming upon the land, if he blows the trumpet and warns the people, then whoever hears the sound of the trumpet and does not take warning, if the sword comes and takes him away, his blood shall be upon his own head. He heard the sound of the trumpet, but did not take warning; his blood shall be upon himself. But he who takes warning will save his life. But if the watchman sees the sword coming and does not blow the trumpet, and the people are not warned, and the sword comes and takes any person from among them, he is taken away in his iniquity; but his blood I will require at the watchman's hand.' So you, son of man: I have made you a watchman

for the house of Israel; therefore you shall hear a word from My mouth and warn them for Me."
EZEKIEL 33:1-7

When you read these words given to Ezekiel, they are sobering. The role that God placed upon him was a serious thing. God appoints Ezekiel as a watchman for the house of Israel. His task is crucial: to hear the word from God's mouth and warn the people. This responsibility was not to be taken lightly, for the consequences were eternal. The watchman had to be vigilant, discerning, and brave enough to sound the alarm when danger was imminent.

A Call for Today's Believers

Today, we live in a time that mirrors the days of Ezekiel in many ways. Our world is rife with hostility, danger, and spiritual warfare. As believers, we are called to be watchmen in our own right. We have been given the task of warning others about the coming judgment and the hope found in Jesus Christ.

Think about it. Just as God commanded Ezekiel to speak to the children of Israel, we too are called to speak to our generation. The sword of judgment is coming, and it is our duty to blow the trumpet of warning. When we see danger, whether it is spiritual deception, moral decay, or outright rebellion against God, we must not remain silent.

The Accountability of a Watchman

In Ezekiel's time, if the watchman failed to blow the trumpet and warn the people, he was held accountable for their blood. This principle applies to us as spiritual watchmen. If we see the impending danger and do not warn others, we bear responsibility.

This is the calling of all pastors, but it doesn't just apply to pastors and leaders. Every believer has a sphere of influence—family, friends, coworkers, and neighbors. We are all watchmen. We must be willing to sound the alarm even when it is unpopular or difficult.

The Urgency of the Message

We live in a time where falsehood permeates not only politics and business but also ministry. False doctrines and misleading teachings are rampant. As watchmen, we must be rooted in the truth of God's Word and be bold in proclaiming it. The trumpet of warning must be loud and clear.

Encouragement and Promise

This task may seem daunting but remember that God equips those He calls. He gives us His Word, His Spirit, and His authority. In Isaiah 41:10, God says, "Fear not, for I am with you; be not dismayed, for I am your God. I will strengthen you, yes, I will help you, I will uphold you with My righteous right hand." This assurance applies to us as well. God promises His strength and help in every task He appoints us to.

Questions for Thought or Discussion

Reflect on Your Role

How can you actively serve as a watchman to this generation?

Sounding the Alarm

Are there situations where you have felt the need to warn others but hesitated? What can you do to overcome that hesitation?

Staying Rooted in Truth

How can you ensure that you are rooted in the truth of God's Word in a world filled with falsehood?

Let's Pray

Heavenly Father,

Thank You for calling us to be watchmen in these times. Help us to stay vigilant and to be bold in proclaiming Your truth. Equip us with the wisdom and courage to sound the alarm and warn others of the dangers ahead. May we be faithful in this responsibility, trusting in Your strength and guidance.

In Jesus' name we pray. Amen.

Day 27

Perspective Adjustment

We walk by faith, not by sight.
2 Corinthians 5:7

If you've ever looked through bifocal glasses, you know that you see things differently when you look through the different layers of the lenses. If you want to see things broad, open, and far away, you look up. If you want to see things up close, magnified, and detailed, you look down. Your perspective matters.

In the book of Esther, we read about how her cousin Mordecai helped her see her situation from a different point of view. Esther had become queen of Persia, but she was initially unaware of the impending danger to her people, the Jews. An evil advisor to the king (Haman) had plotted to annihilate the Jewish population. Mordecai, aware of Esther's position and influence, sent a message to her, saying, "Do not think in your heart that you will escape in the king's palace any more than all the other Jews. For if you remain completely silent at this time, relief and deliverance will arise for the Jews from another place, but you and your father's house will perish. Yet who knows whether you have come to the kingdom for such a time as this?" (Esther 4:13-14)

Up to that point, Esther's focus was nearsighted, concerned primarily with her own safety and position. But Mordecai's words challenged her to see beyond her immediate circumstances. He urged her to understand the reality that her royal position was not just a stroke of fate but a part of God's greater plan for the salvation of her people. This moment shifted Esther's perspective from self-preservation to courageous action, raising her gaze to look at the bigger picture and embrace her role in God's plan.

We are wearing a spiritual version of bifocals. Like Mordecai, I want to make sure that in addition to looking at what's close to you, you are also looking at God's greater plan—especially in these Last Days. I want to make sure you're seeing both views clearly.

Some time ago, I was at Universal Studios theme park. There's a ride where you get on a tram and they tell you, "Before we enter into a certain tunnel, you have to put your glasses on." They give you 3D glasses beforehand to make the experience more realistic.

As we get ready to go into the tunnel, I've already got my glasses on. Everybody at the front of the tram is screaming and freaking out, and I think, "Oh, this sounds like it's going to be good. I can't wait."

It's now our turn to enter the tunnel, and everyone around me is screaming, including my wife, grandkids, and friends. There are dinosaurs spitting at us, King Kong is roaring, and all sorts of stuff is going on, but to be honest, I am underwhelmed. Everything seemed blurry and low-quality to me.

Everyone's ducking and pointing and shouting, "Look out!" and I'm thinking, "I don't get it. This is kind of lame." Once we were out of the tunnel, I started criticizing the ride.

Finally, someone helped me realize that I had been wearing my own sunglasses instead of the 3D glasses. I had been criticizing the ride as a let-down, but it was my own fault that I didn't experience it the way it was intended to be experienced.

Here's the lesson: you have to put on the right glasses and see things the way God intends for you to see them. When you look at the world through the lenses of Scripture, prophecy, and faith, what you see will make so much more sense.

Questions for Thought or Discussion

Perspective

How can you ensure that you are looking at life through the lens of Scripture and faith rather than your own limited perspective?

Broadening Your Vision

In what areas of your life might you be nearsighted, focusing only on the immediate and personal? How can you shift your gaze and broaden your vision so you can see the bigger picture of God's plan?

Correcting Your View

Have you ever experienced a situation where you realized you were not seeing things clearly? How did adjusting your perspective change your understanding?

Let's Pray

Heavenly Father,

Thank You for giving us Your Word and Your Spirit to guide our vision. Help us to see both the immediate and the eternal, the personal and the prophetic. Open our eyes to Your greater plan and purpose for our lives. Give us the wisdom to wear the right spiritual lenses so that we can perceive the world as You intend. May we walk by faith and not by sight, trusting in Your perfect vision.

In Jesus' name we pray. Amen.

Day 28

A Life Worth Dying For

When He opened the fifth seal, I saw under the altar the souls of those who had been slain for the word of God and for the testimony which they held. And they cried with a loud voice, saying, "How long, O Lord, holy and true, until You judge and avenge our blood on those who dwell on the earth?" Then a white robe was given to each of them; and it was said to them that they should rest a little while longer, until both the number of their fellow servants and their brethren, who would be killed as they were, was completed.

Revelation 6:9-11

Who are these people that we read about in Revelation Chapter 6? Are they the Church? No, these are men and women who will face persecution, torture, and ultimately death during the seven-year tribulation period. These tribulation saints will suffer, and their lives will be taken from them because of their steadfast faith in Christ. Unlike those taken up in the Rapture, they have no deliverance from earthly torment. They must die for their faith, and their souls, not their bodies, are immediately brought into the presence of God.

In these verses, we see that these martyrs are very conscious of their surroundings in heaven. They are not in a state of sleep or unconsciousness; they are alert and aware. Their position under the altar signifies that they were sacrificed for their belief in Christ; they are martyrs. The term *slain* used here indicates violence and sacrifice and underscores the brutality and severity of their deaths.

Consider the persecution faced by early Christians and believers throughout history. Think about the Boxer Rebellion, where hundreds of thousands of Christians were martyred. Think about the Soviet Union's brutal repression of believers. During Hitler's regime, not only were six million Jews killed, but an estimated one million Christians who sympathized with Jews also lost their lives. In more recent history, the barbarism of Saddam Hussein included the killings of Christians among his own Kurdish Muslim people. In the Sudan, two million Christians were murdered over a decade.

The tribulation saints' sacrifices are a continuation of history's persecution of God's family, who throughout the ages simply could not deny the transforming power of God in their lives. Despite the brutality they faced, these believers held firm to the Word of God and their testimony. This life of faith in Jesus Christ is a life worth dying for.

The Apostle John, in Revelation 1:9, describes himself as a companion in tribulation and patience of Jesus Christ. He was exiled to the island of Patmos for the Word of God and his testimony. Jesus Himself warned that believers would face hatred and persecution because of their faith in Him. This persecution is a mark of true discipleship and a life transformed by Christ.

The tribulation saints will count the cost of following Christ and will realize the ultimate reward of faithfulness. They cannot deny the change God has wrought in their lives, and this transformation is something every believer experiences and should hold onto in days of trouble. As 2 Corinthians 5:17 states, "Therefore, if anyone is in Christ, he is a new creation; old things have passed away; behold, all things have become new."

Do you know what it is like to have God change your life so profoundly that you cannot deny Him? This is the testimony of the tribulation saints, and it should be the testimony of every believer today. Is this true in your life? Have you experienced such a transformation that you cannot help but hold onto your faith, regardless of the cost?

Are you living a life worth dying for?

Questions for Thought or Discussion

Challenge to Faith

How does the example of the tribulation saints challenge your own faith and commitment to Christ?

Personal Experience

In what ways have you experienced persecution or opposition because of your faith?

Spiritual Preparation

How can you prepare yourself spiritually to stand firm in your faith in the face of increasing hostility?

Let's Pray

Heavenly Father,

Thank You for the powerful testimony of the tribulation saints who will remain faithful even unto death. Help us to have the same steadfast faith and commitment to You. Strengthen us to stand firm in our beliefs, no matter the cost. May we always hold onto Your Word and our testimony of Jesus Christ. In times of trouble and persecution, remind us of Your promise to be with us and to reward our faithfulness.

In Jesus' name we pray. Amen.

Day 29

A Heavenly Wedding

And I heard, as it were, the voice of a great multitude, as the sound of many waters and as the sound of mighty thunderings, saying, "Alleluia! For the Lord God Omnipotent reigns! Let us be glad and rejoice and give Him glory, for the marriage of the Lamb has come, and His wife has made herself ready." And to her it was granted to be arrayed in fine linen, clean and bright, for the fine linen is the righteous acts of the saints.

Revelation 19:6-8

The Bible promises us an incredible wedding—an event that is both awesome and exciting. This is when the Church, referred to as the Bride of Christ, will spiritually and magnificently unite with our Lord Jesus Christ in heaven. For the past 2,000 years, the Church has been engaged to Christ, and this heavenly wedding is the culmination of that relationship.

God the Father, according to the Old Testament, is married to Israel. In a similar yet distinct manner, the Church is engaged to Christ. This future event should fill us with excitement and joy, not apprehension. Weddings are meant to be joyous celebrations, and this ultimate wedding will be the most joyous of all.

Anticipation

Is there anything you're anticipating right now? Something that excites you? Perhaps a vacation, a promotion, or even a wedding? The sense of eager anticipation is probably something you can relate to. But have you ever thought about God being excited about something? We often think of Him as eternally stoic and sober, but the Bible tells us that Jesus is waiting with great anticipation for this heavenly wedding. He is eagerly waiting for the Father to make the announcement. This divine anticipation transcends any excitement we can experience on earth.

    As believers, we should look forward to this event with joy. Revelation 19:6-8 calls us to be glad and rejoice, for the marriage of the Lamb has come. This kind of rejoicing means to jump for joy, to be exuberant with overwhelming happiness. In ancient Middle Eastern culture, weddings were grand, joyful, extended celebrations. Our modern weddings, though significant, often lack the extended celebration and exuberance that were common in biblical times. The wedding of the Lamb, however, is an event that will be filled with unparalleled joy and excitement.

Joy

In Zephaniah 3:17, it says that the Lord will rejoice over you with gladness, and He will quiet you with His love. He will rejoice over you with singing. Imagine the joy in heaven, not only from the saints but from the Lord Himself. This divine joy is something we are called to share in.

As we anticipate this heavenly wedding, let's remember that our ultimate home is in heaven. Nehemiah 8:10 describes the attitude and atmosphere of joy that such a party will evoke: "Go your way, eat the fat, drink the sweet, and send portions to those for whom nothing is prepared; for this day is holy to our Lord. Do not sorrow, for the joy of the Lord is your strength." We can find strength in the joy of the Lord even now, before the wedding, as we focus our thoughts on our Bridegroom. This joy should permeate our lives and remind us daily of the incredible future awaiting us.

Perspective

Revelation 19:7-8 tells us that the Bride has made herself ready, arrayed in fine linen, which represents the righteous acts of the saints. This preparation is a call to live in a manner that honors Christ, reflecting the purity and righteousness that we will fully realize in heaven.

Are you living in holiness, in purity, and in anticipation for your wedding day with Jesus?

Questions for Thought or Discussion

Expectation

How does the promise of a heavenly wedding with Christ shape your view of your relationship with Him?

Joy

Do you experience the kind of joy described in Revelation 19:7-8? If not, what might be hindering you from this joy?

Perspective

How can you remind yourself daily that this earth is not your home and that a joyful, eternal future awaits you?

Let's Pray

Heavenly Father,

Thank You for the promise of the joyous wedding in heaven where we, the Bride of Christ, will unite with our Lord. Help us to live in anticipation of this incredible event, filled with joy and excitement. May we find strength in the joy of the Lord and let it overflow in our daily lives. Prepare our hearts to fully embrace the future You have for us.

In Jesus' name we pray. Amen.

DAY 30

The Lamb Who Is Worthy

"Worthy is the Lamb who was slain
To receive power and riches and wisdom,
And strength and honor and glory and blessing!"
REVELATION 5:12

In the book of Revelation, Jesus is referred to as "the Lamb" 26 times. This title is deeply significant as it reflects His role of the sacrificial Lamb who redeemed us through His blood. The image of the Lamb underscores Jesus' worthiness, sacrifice, and the deep love He demonstrated in laying down His life for us.

The Worthy Lamb

In Revelation 5, John describes a dramatic scene in heaven. A scroll with seven seals is presented, and a mighty angel proclaims with a loud voice, "Who is worthy to open the scroll and to loose its seals?" (Revelation 5:2) There is a profound silence in heaven, as no one in heaven or on the earth or under the earth is able to open the scroll or look at it. John weeps because no one is found worthy. This moment emphasizes the gravity and the significance of the scroll, which represents God's ultimate plan for justice and redemption.

However, one of the elders comforts John, saying, "Do not weep. Behold, the Lion of the tribe of Judah, the Root of David, has prevailed to open the scroll and to loose its seven seals" (Revelation 5:5). When John looks, he sees a lamb, standing as though it had been slain. This juxtaposition of the lion and the lamb reveals the dual nature of Jesus—He is both the conquering king and the sacrificial lamb. The multitude in heaven then proclaims with a loud voice, "Worthy is the Lamb who was slain to receive power and riches and wisdom, and strength and honor and glory and blessing!" (Revelation 5:12) This declaration highlights Jesus' supreme value and honor.

Despite being the King of Kings and Lord of Lords, He chooses to be known as the Lamb. This choice reveals His humility and the depth of His love. His worthiness comes not only from His divine nature but also from His sacrificial death, which secured our redemption.

The Sacrificial Lamb

The Lamb symbolizes Jesus as the ultimate sacrifice for our sins. John the Baptist declared in John 1:29, "Behold! The Lamb of God who takes away the sin of the world!" This speaks to the Old Testament practice of sacrificing lambs to atone for sins. However, Jesus, the

Lamb of God, offered Himself once and for all, ending the need for further sacrifices. His death on the cross was the ultimate act of love and obedience, fulfilling God's plan for our salvation.

The Redeeming Blood

Revelation 12:11 tells us that believers will overcome the great dragon Satan by the blood of the Lamb and the word of their testimony. The blood of Jesus is powerful, redeeming us from sin and securing our victory over evil. It is through His blood that we are cleansed, justified, and reconciled with God.

A Heavenly Wedding

As we anticipate the future, we look forward to the marriage of the Lamb described in Revelation 19. This heavenly wedding is a moment of ultimate joy and celebration. The Bride, the Church, is united with Jesus, the Lamb, in an intimate and eternal relationship.

It's fascinating to note that out of over 700 names for Jesus, He chooses "the Lamb" for the wedding announcement. This name reminds us that our relationship with Him is rooted in His sacrifice. We are here because of the Lamb who took away the sins of the world. The Lamb signifies the cost of our salvation and the love that motivated Jesus to die for us.

In 2 Corinthians 11:2, Paul expresses his godly jealousy for the believers, desiring to present them as a pure Bride to Christ. This imagery reminds us of the importance of remaining faithful and pure in our relationship with Jesus. As we await the heavenly wedding, we are called to live in a manner that honors the Lamb, reflecting His righteousness in our lives.

Questions for Thought or Discussion

Worthiness

How does understanding Jesus as the worthy Lamb deepen your appreciation of His sacrifice?

Sacrifice

What does Jesus' role as the sacrificial Lamb mean to you personally?

Anticipation

How does the anticipation of the heavenly wedding influence your daily walk with Christ?

Let's Pray

Heavenly Father,

Thank You for sending Jesus, the Lamb, to take away our sins. Help us to live in the light of His sacrifice, always mindful of His worthiness and the love He has shown us. As we anticipate the heavenly wedding, may we remain faithful and pure, reflecting the righteousness of the Lamb in our lives. Fill our hearts with joy and excitement for the day we will be united with Jesus forever.

In Jesus' name we pray. Amen.

Day 31

Making the Most of Our Time

Teach us to number our days,
That we may gain a heart of wisdom.
Psalm 90:12

In light of the truth that Jesus Christ could come back at any moment, it is crucial to ask, *What am I doing with my time? Where am I directing my resources? What am I devoting my energy to?*

Time

Time is our most precious commodity. Unlike money or other resources, once time is spent, it cannot be reclaimed. The Bible reminds us of the fleeting nature of time and the importance of using it wisely. Ephesians 5:16 urges us to redeem the time because the days are evil. Every moment is an opportunity to live for God and serve others.

In our busy lives, it's easy to spend time on things that have little eternal value. Consider your daily activities and ask yourself, *Are these pursuits honoring God? Are they helping me grow in faith and love?* While leisure and rest are important, they should not dominate our lives at the expense of spiritual growth and service.

We often find it easier to give money than to give our time. Each of us makes decisions every day to pay for services or conveniences that save us time, because we recognize that time is fleeting. Reflect on whether you are using your time for God's glory or merely for personal convenience. Time is running out, and we must use it wisely, recognizing that our days are numbered and precious.

Resources

Our resources include not just our finances, but also our talents and abilities. 1 Corinthians 10:31 teaches, "Whether you eat or drink, or whatever you do, do all to the glory of God." Everything we have is a gift from God, and we are stewards of these gifts.

Ask yourself, *How am I using my resources for God's glory? Are my financial decisions, career choices, and personal talents being directed toward furthering God's kingdom?* Being a good steward means prioritizing God's purposes over personal gain or comfort.

Vitality

Vitality refers to the energy and life that God has given us. Romans 12:1 encourages us to present our bodies as a *living* sacrifice, holy and acceptable to God. Our physical health and strength are to be used in service to God and others.

Reflect on how you are using your vitality. Are you spending your energy on things that truly matter? Are you investing in relationships, serving those in need, and participating in your church in ways that reflect God's love and truth?

For each of us, the clock will run out and time will be up. For some of us, it could be today or this year. Not so long ago, a woman told me, "I love the Lord, and I've been given a death sentence. I'm going to be with Jesus soon unless He intervenes in my life. There's one thing I regret: I wasted too much time and energy on me. I wish I would've invested more in the things of God." That's powerful.

Our vitality should be dedicated to things of eternal significance. We must use our energy to honor God.

Living as a Light

Jesus said in John 9:4-5, "I must work the works of Him who sent Me while it is day; the night is coming when no one can work. As long as I am in the world, I am the light of the world." As followers of Christ, we are called to be lights in a dark world. Our actions, words, and attitudes should point others to Jesus.

Living this way means being intentional in our witness and striving to honor God in all areas. When we go into the world—our workplace, schools, social events, or errands—we must be a reflection of Christ's love and truth.

Questions for Thought or Discussion

Time

How do you currently spend your time? Are there activities you need to reduce or eliminate to make more time for God?

Resources

In what ways can you use your financial resources more effectively for God's kingdom?

Vitality

What changes can you make to ensure you are using your vitality for God's glory?

Let's Pray

Heavenly Father,

Thank You for the gifts of time, resources, and vitality. Teach us to number our days and use them wisely. Help us to prioritize Your will and live in a way that honors You. Guide us in using our resources for Your glory. Empower us to serve others with the energy and strength You provide. May our lives reflect Your love and truth in all we do.

In Jesus' name we pray. Amen.

Day 32

Witnesses for Christ

"I will give power to my two witnesses, and they will prophesy for 1,260 days, clothed in sackcloth." These are the two olive trees and the two lampstands standing before the God of the earth.
Revelation 11:3-4

In Revelation 11, we read about two extraordinary prophets, ordained and empowered by God to deliver His message for three and a half years. Their ministry is marked by God's protection and miraculous signs. These witnesses, referred to as the two olive trees and the two lampstands standing before the God of the earth, have a crucial role in God's plan during the End Times.

The two witnesses are called to prophesy for 1,260 days, clothed in sackcloth, symbolizing repentance and mourning. God empowers them to shut up the skies from rain, to turn water into blood, and to send plagues upon the earth. They have been given divine authority to speak, and if anyone attempts to harm them, fire proceeds from their mouths and devours their enemies.

Despite their miraculous ministry, the two witnesses are hated by the people, and eventually they are killed. Revelation 11:7 tells us that when they finish their testimony, the beast that ascends from the bottomless pit will make war against them, overcome them, and kill them. Their bodies will lie in the street of the great city for three and a half days, while the world rejoices over them, celebrating their demise by giving gifts to one another.

But after three and a half days, the breath of life from God enters them, and they stand on their feet, terrifying those who see them. Then, they hear a loud voice from heaven saying, "Come up here," and they ascend to heaven in a cloud as their enemies watch. This miraculous resurrection and ascension validates their ministry and glorifies God.

The Call to Be Witnesses

The Greek word for "witness" is *martyr*, indicating one who is dead. As followers of Christ, we are called to be witnesses, dead to ourselves and alive to God's purposes. Romans 12:1-2 encourages us to present our bodies as living sacrifices, holy and acceptable to God. We are to be dead to our old desires and alive to the power of the Holy Spirit.

Just as the two witnesses were empowered by God, we too have the Holy Spirit enabling us to serve God effectively. When we surrender to God, He gives us the strength to overcome anger, perversion, apathy, sin and other struggles. If we are dead to ourselves and alive in Christ, we reflect the object of our worship—Jesus.

Living as a martyr means being fully surrendered to God. It's not about having a death wish but about experiencing the true life that comes from letting go of our own lives and embracing God's will. When we are sold out for Christ, the world becomes a temporary dwelling, and our focus shifts to our eternal home.

Total commitment to God liberates us from the bondage of this world and its worries. It allows us to live with an eternal perspective, focusing on Jesus and His plans for us. God provides the power and strength needed to live out our commitment. When we turn our hearts toward Him, we experience the freedom and joy that come from being His witnesses.

Questions for Thought or Discussion

Witnesses for Christ
How does the ministry and resurrection of the two witnesses inspire you to live as a witness for Christ?

Commitment
What areas do you need to surrender to God so you can be a living sacrifice, holy and acceptable to Him?

Empowerment
How can you rely on the Holy Spirit to give you the strength to overcome and live fully for God?

Let's Pray

Heavenly Father,

Thank You for the example of the two witnesses and their faithful ministry. Help us to live as Your witnesses, fully surrendered to Your will. Empower us by Your Holy Spirit to overcome our struggles and live in a way that reflects Your glory. We want to be living sacrifices, holy and acceptable to You. May our lives point others to the hope we have in Christ.

In Jesus' name we pray. Amen.

Day 33

Rebellion or Surrender?

Behold, He is coming with clouds, and every eye will see Him, even they who pierced Him. And all the tribes of the earth will mourn because of Him. Even so, Amen.

REVELATION 1:7

Jesus Christ is coming back again! The anticipation of His second coming is both awe-inspiring and sobering. Revelation 19:19 presents a vivid and astonishing scene: "And I saw the beast, the kings of the earth, and their armies, gathered together to make war against Him who sat on the horse and against His army." Christ's return will reveal an immense rebellion of humanity against God, led by the Antichrist and supported by the kings and armies of the earth. This physical battle is the culmination of the ongoing spiritual battle that has raged through the centuries.

The Outrageous Rebellion

Consider the audacity of humanity to turn their weapons against Jesus Christ Himself. The Antichrist, the future world leader, Satan's consummate politician who will arise from a revived Roman Empire, will deceive many and consolidate power, leading to this climactic battle.

Despite the miraculous signs and wonders that will precede Jesus' return, many will refuse to believe and will instead unite in rebellion against Him. It is astonishing to think that even as the heavens rumble and Christ appears, the nations will choose to fight against Him rather than surrender. This rebellion underscores the hardness of the human heart and the deception that blinds many to the truth.

Following Christ Now

In light of this future rebellion, we must ask ourselves, *Are we willing to follow Christ now while we have the opportunity?* Jesus' words in John 10:27-28 speak to this: "My sheep hear My voice, and I know them, and they follow Me. And I give them eternal life, and they shall never perish; neither shall anyone snatch them out of My hand." As His sheep, we are called to recognize His voice and follow Him faithfully.

This call to follow Christ is not without challenges. It requires us to deny ourselves, take up our cross, and follow Him daily (Matthew 16:24-26). Each of us has a unique cross to bear, whether it is past wounds, difficult relationships, or specific callings that stretch our faith. Jesus invites us to trust Him with our lives, to let go of our own plans, and to embrace His will.

Worshiping in Spirit and Truth

As we read about the future events described in Revelation, we must remember the importance of worshiping God in spirit and truth. The idolatry and false worship that will characterize the End Times stand in stark contrast to the pure and holy worship that God desires. Jesus emphasized in John 4:23-24 that true worshipers will worship the Father in spirit and truth, for the Father is seeking such to worship Him.

Our worship must be genuine and grounded in the truth of God's Word. It is not about external rituals or visible idols, but about a heart that is fully devoted to God. This kind of worship honors God and aligns our lives with His plans.

Rebellion or Surrender?

We all have rebellion inside of us. The rebellion in our hearts is exemplified by the final battle in Revelation, where humanity's defiance reaches its peak. Yet, we have the choice to surrender to Christ, letting go of that rebellion and choosing His way. When we yield to His will, we embrace a life of purpose and peace, walking in the better path that He has set before us.

Questions for Thought or Discussion

Self-Denial

Are you willing to follow Christ wholeheartedly, even when it requires self-denial and sacrifice?

True Worship

How can you deepen your worship of God, ensuring it is rooted in spirit and truth?

Faithfulness

How can you remain vigilant and faithful, anticipating the return of Jesus Christ?

Let's Pray

Heavenly Father,

Thank You for the promise of Jesus' return. Help us to live in anticipation of that day, giving all that we have and relinquishing all that we are for Your glory. Strengthen our faith and help us to follow Christ wholeheartedly, bearing our unique crosses with grace and trust. Guide us to worship You in spirit and truth, avoiding the idols of this world. Keep us vigilant and faithful, ready for Your coming.

In Jesus' name we pray. Amen.

Day 34

The Coming Millennium

Unto us a Child is born,
Unto us a Son is given;
And the government will be upon His shoulder.
And His name will be called Wonderful, Counselor,
Mighty God, Everlasting Father, Prince of Peace.
Of the increase of His government and peace
There will be no end,
Upon the throne of David and over His kingdom,
To order it and establish it with judgment
and justice
From that time forward, even forever.
The zeal of the Lord of hosts will perform this.

Isaiah 9:6-7

The word *millennium*, in Latin, means "a thousand years." The term is used to describe the reign of Jesus Christ after His second coming. According to Scripture, after Jesus returns to earth, He will establish His kingdom, ruling and reigning from Jerusalem for a thousand years.

Isaiah 9:6-7 describes this future reign vividly. While we often hear Isaiah 9:6 to celebrate the birth of Christ at Christmas, the prophecy also speaks of a time when He will govern with wisdom, justice, and peace. Currently, Jesus is in heaven with the Father, not yet seated on David's throne in Zion. The fulfillment of this portion of the Scripture is still to come and will take place during the millennium. Isaiah 65 and Zechariah 14 give us a glimpse into what this millennium will look like.

Isaiah 65:17-25 paints a beautiful picture of life during this period. God promises to create new heavens and a new earth, with Jerusalem as a place of joy. There will be no more weeping or distress. Lifespans will be extended, and people will live in harmony and prosperity. The natural world will also be transformed: "The wolf and the lamb shall feed together, the lion shall eat straw like an ox" (v. 25). This vision reflects a restored creation, free from violence and pain.

Zechariah 14:16-19 adds that all nations will come to Jerusalem annually to worship the King, the Lord of hosts. Those who do not come will face consequences, which emphasizes the importance of honoring God. This period will be marked by reverence and dedication to the Lord, with even the bells on horses inscribed with "Holiness to the Lord."

The millennial kingdom will usher in a time of unparalleled peace, justice, and divine presence. Jesus will rule as a righteous monarch, fulfilling the promises made to David and bringing God's kingdom to earth in a tangible way. It's hard to imagine how amazing it will be, but fun to try!

Who will be living in this millennium? According to the Bible, those who survive the Tribulation will enter the millennium as mortals, and they will repopulate the earth. Isaiah indicates that people will live much longer, with children being considered youthful at a hundred years old. This extended longevity reflects the restored and flourishing state of the earth under Jesus' reign. Despite the dramatic population reduction caused by the devastation of the Tribulation, the earth will be repopulated and blossom beautifully.

Additionally, believers who have been faithful will reign with Christ during this period. Revelation 20:4-6 explains that we will rule and reign alongside Jesus. In our glorified bodies, free from sin, we will execute justice and righteousness. While mortals born during the millennium will still have the propensity to sin, those of us reigning with Christ will help to uphold His perfect justice.

As we watch and wait for the Lord's return, we also anticipate a world where He rules and reigns. The governments of this world are broken and corrupt, but God will rule with true justice and unsurpassed peace.

Questions for Thought or Discussion

Reflect

How does the promise of Jesus' future reign impact your understanding of current world events?

Prepare

In what ways can you prepare your heart and life for the coming of Christ's kingdom?

Apply

How can the vision of the millennial kingdom inspire you to live a life of holiness and dedication to God now?

Let's Pray

Heavenly Father,

Thank You for the promise of Your Son's return and His righteous reign on earth. Help us to live in anticipation of that glorious day, aligning our lives with Your will and embracing the peace and justice that Your kingdom represents. May we be agents of Your love and righteousness in the world today, reflecting the harmony and holiness of the future kingdom.

In Jesus' name we pray. Amen.

Day 35

The Binding of Satan

> Then I saw an angel coming down from heaven, having the key to the bottomless pit and a great chain in his hand. He laid hold of the dragon, that serpent of old, who is the Devil and Satan, and bound him for a thousand years.
>
> Revelation 20:1-2

In these verses, John describes an unforgettable moment when an angel comes down from heaven with the key to the bottomless pit and a great chain. This angel's mission is to seize Satan, bind him, and cast him into the abyss, locking him away for a thousand years. Some interpret this angel as Jesus Christ, but the text simply refers to "an angel," suggesting it could be any angelic being. The focus is not on the angel's identity but on the authority and power granted to carry out God's command.

The binding of Satan signifies a significant shift in the spiritual realm. During the millennium that follows this event, the devil will no longer deceive the nations. This period will be characterized by peace, justice, and divine governance, as Jesus Christ will reign as the righteous monarch from the throne of David in Zion.

As the angel lays hold of Satan and binds him, the picture the Greek text gives is of winding something tight around him or placing a straitjacket on him. The imagery of binding and loosing has significant spiritual implications. Just as the angel binds Satan, we must consider the things in our lives that keep us bound.

Satan's influence is evident in the world through sin, deception, and suffering. As believers, we are often caught in the web of these lies, bound by fear, doubt, and temptation. But just as the angel has the power to bind Satan, we have been given the power through Christ to break free from the chains of sin and live in the freedom He provides.

Remember the account of Lazarus in John 11. When Jesus called Lazarus out of the tomb, he emerged bound in graveclothes. Jesus commanded, "Loose him, and let him go" (v. 44). This command is not just about physical freedom but spiritual liberation. Many of us, although alive in Christ, still wear the graveclothes of our past sins and fears. Jesus calls us to shed these bindings and live fully in His freedom.

Sin and deception are tools Satan uses to keep us bound. Jesus said in John 8:44 that Satan is the father of lies and a murderer from the beginning. The first murder was not with a sword or a knife but with a lie that killed Adam and Eve spiritually. This deception continues today, but we have the truth of God's Word to set us free.

The key to living free from these bindings is found in the Word of God. By immersing ourselves in Scripture, we can combat the lies of the enemy and embrace the truth that sets us free. Jesus declared in John 8:32, "You shall know the truth, and the truth shall make you free."

As we anticipate the binding of Satan and the ultimate reign of Christ, let's also focus on the freedom available to us now through Jesus. We don't have to wait for the millennium to experience liberation from sin. The power that will bind Satan is the same power that can free us today.

Questions for Thought or Discussion

Bondage
What are some areas in your life where you feel bound or restricted by sin or fear?

Freedom
How can immersing yourself in God's Word help you to break free from these bindings?

Action
What steps can you take to live in the freedom that Christ offers and shed the graveclothes of your past?

Let's Pray

Heavenly Father,

Thank You for the promise of Satan's ultimate defeat and the freedom we have in Christ. Help us to live in that freedom every day, breaking free from the sins and fears that bind us. Fill us with Your truth and empower us to walk boldly in Your light. May we shed the graveclothes of our past and embrace the new life You offer.

In Jesus' name we pray. Amen.

Day 36

When We Come Home

I saw a new heaven and a new earth, for the first heaven and the first earth had passed away. Also there was no more sea.

Revelation 21:1

In Revelation 21:1-8, we are given a magnificent vision of the future, where God promises a new heaven and a new earth. This passage is filled with hope and assurance, describing the ultimate fulfillment of God's plan for His creation and His people.

When we think about coming home, we often imagine a joyous reunion with loved ones, a time of catching up and renewing relationships. This concept of a homecoming is a picture of what the Lord has in store for us. When we come home to Him, everything will be new. The old, marred by sin and suffering, will pass away, and a new, perfect creation will take its place.

The vision begins with John seeing a new heaven and a new earth because the first heaven and earth had passed away. The need for this renewal is evident in the world around us, groaning under the weight of sin. As

Isaiah 65:17 declares, "For behold, I create new heavens and a new earth; and the former shall not be remembered or come to mind." The promise of a new creation free from the corruption and decay of the present world fills us with hope and longing.

John also sees the holy city, New Jerusalem, descending from heaven, prepared as a bride adorned for her husband. This imagery of a bride signifies purity, beauty, and joy. The New Jerusalem will be the focal point of eternity, where God Himself will dwell with His people. 1 Corinthians 2:9-10 tells us that no eye has seen, no ear has heard, nor has it entered into the heart of man what God has prepared for those who love Him. This city represents the ultimate fulfillment of God's promise to be with us and to be our God.

As we move further into the passage, we hear a loud voice from heaven proclaiming that the tabernacle of God is with men, and He will dwell with them. Faith will no longer be needed because we will see God face to face. The temporary struggles of this life will give way to the eternal joy of His presence. John 14:2-3 reassures us that Jesus has gone to prepare a place for us, and He will come again to receive us to Himself. Our eternal home will be one of perfect fellowship with God.

God will wipe away every tear from our eyes, and there will be no more death, sorrow, crying, or pain. The former things will pass away. The removal of the curse that began in the Garden of Eden (Genesis 3:17-19) will restore God's original desire for humanity to be blessed and happy. Psalm 16:11 reminds us that in God's presence, there is fullness of joy and eternal pleasures. Our present sufferings, though real and painful, are achieving for us an eternal glory that far outweighs them all (2 Corinthians 4:17).

In this new creation, the past will be left behind. The burdens, pain, and sins of this world will be no more. This is the future that awaits us in Christ: a future where we can fully experience the joy and peace of God's presence, unburdened by the troubles of this life.

The passage in Revelation 21 concludes with God proclaiming from His throne, "Behold, I make all things new" (v. 5). His words are true and faithful, affirming the certainty of His promise. He declares, "It is done! I am the Alpha and the Omega, the Beginning and the End" (v. 6). And He will freely give the water of life to those who thirst, signifying eternal satisfaction and fulfillment in Him.

What a future awaits those who are followers of Jesus Christ!

Questions for Thought or Discussion

Future Hope
How does the promise of a new heaven and a new earth inspire hope in your daily life?

Present Presence

In what ways can you experience the presence of God now, anticipating the perfect fellowship to come?

Eternal Glory

How can you shift your focus from temporary struggles to the eternal glory that awaits in God's perfect kingdom?

Let's Pray

Heavenly Father,

Thank You for the promise of a new heaven and earth. Help us to live in anticipation of that glorious day, keeping our eyes fixed on Jesus. Strengthen our faith and help us to overcome the challenges we face, knowing that our future with You is secure. Guide us to live in Your presence now and prepare us for the joy of eternal fellowship with You.

In Jesus' name we pray. Amen.

Day 37

The River of Life

He showed me a pure river of water of life, clear as crystal, proceeding from the throne of God and of the Lamb. In the middle of its street, and on either side of the river, was the tree of life, which bore twelve fruits, each tree yielding its fruit every month. The leaves of the tree were for the healing of the nations. And there shall be no more curse, but the throne of God and of the Lamb shall be in it, and His servants shall serve Him. They shall see His face, and His name shall be on their foreheads. There shall be no night there: They need no lamp nor light of the sun, for the Lord God gives them light. And they shall reign forever and ever.

Revelation 22:1-5

Revelation 22 holds a special place in my heart because I first read it on the night I got saved. After hearing the gospel and responding to the call, the new convert counselors at Calvary Chapel Costa Mesa handed me a brand-new New Testament. Being an impatient person,

I didn't start reading from the beginning. Instead, I did what I always do when I get a book: I read the last chapter first. I wanted to know how it was going to end. And so, I opened up to Revelation 22 and read about the river of life.

Revelation 22:1-5 describes a pure river of water of life, clear as crystal, flowing from the throne of God and of the Lamb. This river represents the sufficiency of God that is in Christ. It symbolizes a life-giving force that flows from God's throne. Along with the river, we read about the tree of life which bears twelve kinds of fruit, yielding its fruit every month, and the leaves of the tree are for the healing of the nations.

Zig Ziglar coined the phrase "win-win situation," and that's what comes to mind when I read the last chapter of Revelation. Following Christ is a win-win scenario. If we live for Christ, we win in this life because we have His guidance, peace, and joy. And if we die, we win by entering directly into His presence and enjoying eternity in heaven with Him. As Paul said, "For to me, to live is Christ, and to die is gain" (Philippians 1:21).

The river of life in Revelation is not just ordinary water. It is a symbol of the eternal life and fulfillment found in God. This river flows from the very throne of God, emphasizing that the source of true life and satisfaction is Him. Jesus repeated this truth in John 7:37-38, where He said, "If anyone thirsts, let him come to Me and drink. He who believes in Me, as the

Scripture has said, out of his heart will flow rivers of living water."

This invitation from Jesus is a call to experience the abundant life that only He can provide. We cannot attain this life through our efforts, good deeds, or wealth. It is a gift from God, available to all who are willing to receive it. Our ultimate satisfaction and joy come from Christ alone.

In Revelation 22, we also see that there will be no more curse. The throne of God and of the Lamb will be in the city, and His servants will serve Him. They shall see His face, and His name shall be on their foreheads. There will be no night there, no need for a lamp or the light of the sun, for the Lord God will give them light, and they shall reign forever and ever.

This vision of the future fills us with hope and anticipation. It encourages us to live with eternity in mind, knowing that our ultimate destination is a place of perfect peace and fulfillment in God's presence.

Questions for Thought or Discussion

Our New Home
What is your favorite part of the description of your eternal home found in the final chapters of Revelation?

God's Sufficiency
How does the promise of the River of Life affect your understanding of God's provision and sufficiency?

Application

How can you live in a way that reflects the abundant life Jesus offers? How can you share this life with others?

Let's Pray

Heavenly Father,

Thank You for the promise of the river of life and the eternal fulfillment it symbolizes. Help us to understand and embrace the abundant life that only You can provide. Help us live each day with the assurance of Your sufficiency and the hope of seeing You face to face. Guide us to share this life-giving water with those around us, reflecting Your love in all we do.

In Jesus' name we pray. Amen.

Day 38

Face to Face

They shall see His face, and His name shall be on their foreheads. There shall be no night there: They need no lamp nor light of the sun, for the Lord God gives them light. And they shall reign forever and ever.

Revelation 22:4-5

Can you imagine the sheer awe and excitement of seeing God face to face? Throughout the Bible, no one has ever seen the face of God. However, the promise in Revelation 22:4-5 is that we, the redeemed, will one day behold the face of God. This is an anticipation that should fill our hearts with incredible joy and hope.

Do you remember the story of Moses and how he wanted to see God in all His glory? In Exodus, Moses fervently desired to see God. He persistently asked God to show His glory. God's response was both tender and firm: "You cannot see My face; for no man shall see Me, and live" (Exodus 33:20).

But God granted Moses his request to the extent that Moses could withstand. God placed Moses in the cleft of a rock, covered him with His hand, passed by the cleft, and allowed him to see only His afterglow. Even this brief glimpse was so powerful that Moses' face shone with divine radiance. He had to wear a veil to cover the glow that shone from his face caused from seeing the aftereffects of God's glory.

Imagine the scene: Moses, the great leader of Israel, standing on Mount Sinai, enveloped by God's presence. The mountain quaked, and smoke billowed as God descended in fire. Moses, filled with a holy curiosity and longing, dared to ask God to reveal His glory. God's compassion for Moses is evident as He makes provision for Moses to experience His presence in a safe way. God's hand shielding Moses was both a protection and a loving gesture. When God removed His hand, Moses saw the afterglow, a mere reflection of God's passing glory. This encounter was so intense that when Moses descended the mountain, his face radiated with light, reflecting the divine encounter, and the Israelites were afraid to come near him (Exodus 34:29-35).

What would Moses have thought if he had access to the full revelation of Scripture that we have today? He would have read Revelation 22:4 with awe and longing. Moses, who only saw the afterglow of God, would have been astounded to know that the redeemed will one day see God face to face. This desire to see God is a fundamental longing of the human heart. The psalmist expressed it beautifully in Psalm 27:4: "One thing I have desired of the Lord, that will I seek: that I may dwell in the house of the Lord all the days of my life, to behold the beauty of the Lord."

The New Testament affirms this hope. Paul writes in 1 Corinthians 13:12, "For now we see in a mirror, dimly, but then face to face. Now I know in part, but then I shall know just as I also am known." Similarly, Jesus in Matthew 5:8 promises, "Blessed are the pure in heart, for they shall see God." This promise finds its ultimate fulfillment in Revelation 22:4.

When we see God face to face, we will experience His presence in a way that surpasses all current understanding. It will be an eternal communion with the Creator, in a place where there is no night, no need for artificial light or even the sun, for God Himself will be our light. This eternal communion will fulfill our deepest longings.

Living in the light of this promise should transform how we live today. The anticipation of seeing God face to face encourages us to pursue purity and holiness, knowing that our ultimate reward is not just a place in heaven but a personal, intimate relationship with God Himself.

Questions for Thought or Discussion

Longing

What does the promise of seeing God face to face mean to you personally?

Transformation

How does this future reality impact your current walk with God?

Expectation

In what ways can you live today in anticipation of that glorious day when you will see God face to face?

Let's Pray

Heavenly Father,

We are overwhelmed by the promise that we will one day see You face to face. Thank You for this incredible hope that sustains us and gives us joy. Help us to live in purity and anticipation, reflecting Your glory in our lives. May we seek Your presence daily and long for the day when we will behold Your face and dwell in Your eternal light.

In Jesus' name we pray. Amen.

Day 39

No More, No Less

I testify to everyone who hears the words of the prophecy of this book: If anyone adds to these things, God will add to him the plagues that are written in this book; and if anyone takes away from the words of the book of this prophecy, God shall take away his part from the Book of Life, from the holy city, and from the things which are written in this book.

Revelation 22:18-19

In the closing chapter of Revelation, John delivers a solemn warning about the integrity of God's Word. These final words, spoken by the Holy Spirit and recorded by John, emphasize the sacredness of the biblical text. As followers of Christ, we are called to handle Scripture with reverence, ensuring we neither add to nor subtract from its teachings. This call to vigilance is more pressing today than ever before, as false teachings proliferate and seek to dilute the truth of God's Word.

The Sacred Integrity of Scripture

The warning in Revelation 22:18-19 speaks to God's jealousy for His Word. To tamper with Scripture is to tamper with divine revelation. Psalm 138:2 tells us that God exalts His Word above His name, highlighting the profound respect we must have for the Bible. Adding to or subtracting from the Word is not merely an error but a serious transgression with dire consequences.

In our age, there are numerous voices attempting to distort the message of the Bible. From interpretations that align more with cultural trends than biblical truth to outright additions and deletions of Scripture, the integrity of God's Word is under constant attack. This makes our commitment to knowing and upholding the Bible in its entirety crucial.

False Prophets and Cults

Today, false prophets and cults are more prevalent than ever. They add to the Bible, creating new doctrines and gospels that lead many astray. They also subtract from it, dismissing or reinterpreting passages to fit their agendas. Jesus Himself warned of such deception, urging us to stay vigilant and grounded in the truth.

In Galatians 1:8-9, Paul wrote, "But even if we, or an angel from heaven, preach any other gospel to you than what we have preached to you, let him be accursed. As we have said before, so now I say again, if anyone preaches any other gospel to you than what you have received, let him be accursed."

It is crucial that we adhere strictly to the apostolic teaching handed down to us.

Knowing Our Bibles

To guard against deception, we must know our Bibles thoroughly. Hebrews 1:1-2 tells us that God has spoken to us through His Son in these Last Days, and the Bible is the recorded revelation of His will. "God, who at various times and in various ways spoke in time past to the fathers by the prophets, has in these last days spoken to us by His Son, whom He has appointed heir of all things, through whom also He made the worlds."

The Holy Spirit, the true author of Scripture, has given us a complete and all-sufficient Word. Our task is to study it, understand it, and live by it. We should put the Bible into practice daily. By immersing ourselves in Scripture, we can discern truth from falsehood and stand firm in our faith. This requires a disciplined approach, reading, meditating on, and applying God's Word consistently.

Questions for Thought or Discussion

Scriptural Integrity

How can you ensure that you are not adding to or taking away from the teachings of the Bible in your understanding and application?

Vigilance Against False Teachings

Are you aware of the false teachings and cults prevalent today? How can you guard yourself against them?

Daily Practice

How can you incorporate more regular and intentional Bible study into your daily life?

Let's Pray

Heavenly Father,

Thank You for the gift of Your Word, which is a lamp to our feet and a light to our path. Help us to handle Scripture with the utmost reverence, neither adding to nor taking away from its truth. Give us discernment to recognize false teachings and strength to stand firm in Your Word. Empower us to study, meditate on, and apply the Bible in our daily lives, that we may live according to Your will. We eagerly await the return of our Lord Jesus Christ and pray that Your grace and mercy be with us until that Day.

In Jesus' name we pray. Amen.

Day 40

Come!

> "Behold, I am coming quickly, and My reward is with Me, to give to every one according to his work. I am the Alpha and the Omega, the Beginning and the End, the First and the Last."
> Revelation 22:12-13

Chances are, if you have reached Day 40 of a devotional book like this, you are already a believer. But it may be that you are reading this, and you realize you have just been pretending. Perhaps you've stumbled onto this book, or it was a gift, and you have been reading about all of these End Times events with fascination, but you don't know Jesus—the One this is all about.

Will you come to Christ now? Please, will you? Will you open your heart today? Will you take a stand and decide to give up everything for Christ? This plea is for your sake—for you to begin a relationship with Jesus.

The Call to Surrender

Perhaps you have attended church for years. Your name might be on the roll of church accomplishments, and you might contribute regularly. But have you truly surrendered your heart to Christ? This is not about religiosity; it's about a personal relationship with Jesus.

Jesus, speaking in Revelation 22:12-13, declares that He is coming quickly and will reward everyone according to their work. He is the Alpha and the Omega, the Beginning and the End, the First and the Last. This announcement is both a warning and a comfort. It's a call to examine our lives and decide if we have truly come to Christ, leaving behind all pretenses and self-righteousness.

Jesus' Invitation

In Revelation 22:16-17, Jesus says, "I, Jesus, have sent My angel to testify to you these things in the churches. I am the Root and the Offspring of David, the Bright and Morning Star. And the Spirit and the bride say, 'Come!' And let him who hears say, 'Come!' And let him who thirsts come. Whoever desires, let him take the water of life freely."

Jesus extends an open invitation to all who hear. He calls us to come and receive the water of life freely. This invitation is not about joining a church denomination or adhering to a set of rules. It's about coming to Jesus with a humble heart, asking Him to forgive you of your sin, acknowledging your need for Him, and accepting His gift of salvation.

The Urgency of His Return

Jesus' promise to return is mentioned multiple times in the Scriptures. (See Titus 2:13, 1 Thessalonians 1:10, Hebrews 9:28, Philippians 3:20, 1 Corinthians 1:7, and Jude 1:21.) This serves as a comforting promise to the Church.

"Behold, I am coming quickly" carries two significant meanings. First, it means that Jesus could come at any moment. His return will be unexpected, catching many off guard. Second, when He does come, it will happen rapidly. The events surrounding His return will unfold quickly and decisively. Both of these statements emphasize the need for readiness and vigilance in our spiritual lives.

Living in Readiness

This understanding should motivate us to live in a state of constant readiness. Our daily lives should reflect an expectation of Jesus' imminent return. We should be diligent in our faith, steadfast in our commitment, and determined in our obedience to His commands. The promise of His quick return is not just a warning but a source of comfort and hope for those who are faithful.

To learn more about beginning a relationship with Jesus Christ, please visit **jackhibbs.com/know-god**. It would be my pleasure to send you a free Bible and resources that can help you grow in faith and learn more about God and His Word.

Questions for Thought or Discussion

Personal Surrender

Have you truly surrendered your heart to Christ, leaving behind all forms of self-righteousness and religious pretenses?

Heeding the Invitation

How have you responded to Jesus' invitation to come and drink of the water of life freely?

Living in Readiness

Are you living in a way that reflects readiness for Christ's sudden return?

Let's Pray

Heavenly Father,

Thank You for the open invitation to come to You and receive the water of life freely. Help us to lay aside all pretenses and self-righteousness, surrendering fully to Your will. May we live in readiness for Jesus' return, understanding the urgency and significance of His promise. Fill our hearts with a deep desire to know You and follow You wholeheartedly.

In Jesus' name we pray. Amen.

About the Author

JACK HIBBS is the senior and founding pastor of Calvary Chapel Chino Hills in Southern California. He is also the host of the nationally syndicated TV and radio program *Real Life*, and his daily media programs reach millions worldwide. Jack and his wife, Lisa, have two adult daughters and three grandchildren.

Discover more of Jack's teachings and resources at **jackhibbs.com**.